YES!
You Can Learn a
Foreign Language

Marjory Brown-Azarowicz

Charlotte Stannard

Mark Goldin

PASSPORT BOOKS
a division of *NTC Publishing Group*
Lincolnwood, Illinois USA

For Ana, Calvin, Diane, Ginger, John,
Kathy, Michael, Michele, Susan, and
Warren.

Published by Passport Books, a division of NTC Publishing Group.
© 1989 by NTC Publishing Group, 4255 West Touhy Avenue,
Lincolnwood (Chicago), Illinois 60646-1975 U.S.A.
Manufactured in the United States of America.

8 9 0 ML 9 8 7 6 5 4 3 2 1

Contents

Preface

This book is for you, the high school, adult, or college student who is studying a new language. It is designed to help you get started learning a new language, establish your goals, and achieve them. It may also be used as a resource book by counselors, teachers, and parents who want to help learners study languages effectively.

At the Study Skills Center on our college campus, students ask for help in foreign languages more often than in any other discipline. Because so many learners experience problems, and because few resources are available to help with foreign language study skills, this book has been written to bring together successful study ideas based on contemporary research, as well as ideas from our experiences with learners.

The most frequent learning problems are related to learners' attitudes toward foreign language study. Learners may not perceive the relevance of foreign languages to their lives, and they may have negative attitudes toward anything foreign. Problems associated with attitudes seem to underlie other academic problems such as inability to organize time effectively, difficulty in memorizing, fear of speaking in class, and difficulties in motivating oneself for long-term commitment to language learning.

The main reason why many North Americans have negative attitudes about foreign language study is cultural ethnocentrism. Americans have often felt uncomfortable with the idea of studying a new culture and language. Historically, the immigrant to America was expected to transform himself or herself into an American, but an immigrant would always be an incomplete American ''who still carried the stigma of Europe in his broken accent and ways of living.

As a first-generation American, he had only managed to climb halfway...because his ties to the Old World kept him from completely embracing the new way of life."[1]

The second-generation American rejected the values and culture of first-generation Americans and tried to be "a one hundred per cent American, intolerant of anything foreign." Successive generations of Americans have been affected by the negative attitudes of their parents toward all things foreign, including languages. American society, as a whole, has encouraged conformity to the melting pot concept in which diverse peoples become one nation. To participate in the American dream, one must reject the old cultures. Foreign language study is part of what is rejected.

Although some of these old ideas persist, we are in an age of pluralism in society and of increased communication among nations and people. Recent events, such as the earthquake in Mexico and the severe drought in Ethiopia, have illustrated that we are not only citizens of our nation, but citizens of the world as well. Foreign language study and a knowledge of other cultures are probably more important now than at any other time in history. But whether a student pursues goals of a universal or a personal nature, success in learning a foreign language is truly attainable.

Each learner must personally come to terms with the cultural conflicts inherent in foreign language study. Each learner should also come to terms with the study skills that promote successful language learning. This book is designed to show you how you can overcome the problems involved in foreign language study and what you can do to study successfully.

The chapters of this book are written in a practical way with ideas intended to help you in your studies every day. The first three chapters are about you as a language learner. Chapters 1 and 2 help you form the attitudes that will assist you more than anything else with the task of language learning. Chapter 3 is about memorization and offers a wealth of suggestions for developing your memory for learning the vocabulary and other elements of your new language.

---

[1] Paul R. Turner, "Why Johnny Doesn't Want to Learn a Foreign Language," *Modern Language Journal* 58 (1974):192. This is a paraphrase of Margaret Mead, *And Keep Your Powder Dry* (New York: William Morrow & Co., 1942), p. 47. The quotation in the next paragraph is also from Turner.

The second group of three chapters is concerned with your new language itself. These chapters suggest ways to be successful in listening, speaking, reading, and writing in your new language. If you are learning a language that does not use the familiar Latin alphabet, Chapter 5 will help you in learning a new writing system.

Chapters 7 through 9 are concerned with elements that are external to you and to your new language but that may still affect your learning. The most important of these is your instructor, so Chapter 7 explains how you can get the best help possible from a foreign language teacher. If you are enrolled in a formal language course in which you will be evaluated, you will want to know about the test-taking skills in Chapter 8. Chapter 9 notes some of the products of technology that can support your language learning.

A final chapter, entitled "Survival and Success," has been written to help and encourage you to survive the ups and downs of long-term study and to keep working until you reach your goals.

Appendix A, "A Word to Counselors and Teachers," addresses the people who can most effectively provide support and guidance to the language learner. Appendix B is an annotated bibliography of recommended reading.

A large part of this book is about the role that the support, encouragement, and assistance of others can play in learning. These factors have played no small part for us in writing, so we would like to express appreciation to National Textbook Company, and especially to our editor, Michael Ross, for providing encouragement, support, and assistance in making this volume a reality.

M.B.A.
M.G.G.
C.M.S.

Fairfax, Virginia

1

Getting Started

You probably have several reasons for learning a new language. You may want to travel abroad and believe that knowing a new language will make your trip more enjoyable. You may need to learn a new language because it is required for college or to get a job. You may wish to acquire proficiency in a new language in order to use your knowledge in a career with the government, in international business, or in education. Or you may want to work as a translator, teacher, salesperson, interpreter, or tour guide. No matter what your objectives may be, this book takes the viewpoint that you are going to understand, speak, read, and write a new language and that you want to be successful in these endeavors.

CHOOSING YOUR GOALS

To be successful in learning a new language, it is important to spend a little time thinking about why you want to study the language. On the next page there is a questionnaire that will help you analyze your goals and your commitment to the study of a new language. Answer the questions, total your scores, and assess your total commitment.

RATE YOUR COMMITMENT TO STUDYING A NEW LANGUAGE

Please rate yourself. Follow the directions with each question to rate your commitment to learning a new language.

Score

Personal Goals

1. Why do you want to learn a new language? What rewards will this bring? For every reason you state, give yourself 1 point. (Maximum: 5)   ___

2. In comparison with your other activities, how important is learning a new language? (1: of little importance; 2: of average importance; 3: very important)   ___

3. How much do you want to be like the people who speak the language you wish to learn? (1: I do not want to be like them in any way; 2: I wouldn't mind adopting some of their ways and ideas; 3: I admire them and would like to be able to act as they do.)   ___

Personal Attitudes

4. If you have previously had a positive learning experience in a new language, give yourself 2 points.   ___

5. If you are the sort of person who will try something new and not be disturbed by your mistakes, give yourself 3 points. If you become somewhat upset when you make mistakes, give yourself 2 points. If you cannot stand to make mistakes, especially in front of others, give yourself 1 point or zero.   ___

Time and Money

6. Your chances of success will be increased if you know in advance the time and cost involved in your study. If you will have sufficient time and money for your language study, give yourself 2 points.   ___

Add your total score: ___

Key

If you scored 13 or higher, you are very likely to succeed because of your strong commitment to the study of your new language. If you scored 8 to 12, you are quite likely to succeed. If you scored below 8, you need to reevaluate your objectives, or your time and financial commitments, or your attitudes toward the study of this new language.

What rating did you receive? How strong is your present commitment? You may find that as you progress in your new language, your commitment and interest will grow. As you set objectives for yourself, and reach each one, you will want to go on and learn more. You will know when you have reached your ultimate personal goal for proficiency in your new language because you will be satisfied with your accomplishments, and your knowledge of the new language will meet your personal, professional, or social needs.

LEVELS OF LANGUAGE PROFICIENCY

Language study is a long-term activity in which you pass through various stages or levels of proficiency. The American Council on the Teaching of Foreign Languages has developed definitions of proficiency levels which you may use to determine your present level. Whether you already have some ability in a foreign language or are beginning from scratch, you can use these definitions to help you set your objectives at the level of proficiency you one day wish to reach.

Novice Level

At the first, novice level of proficiency, you are able to use two- or three-word expressions such as "hello"; "goodbye"; "Where is the bus?" Your pronunciation sounds much like your first language. When listening to others, you understand the words and phrases you have memorized, such as simple questions and statements about the names, addresses, and ages of family members, as well as the weather, time, and daily activities. You can read words you have learned such as those on menus, schedules, timetables, maps, and signs. You can write names, numbers, dates, addresses, learned vocabulary, phrases, and simple lists using the symbols of an alphabet or other system. This level is attained usually with less than 100 hours of instructional time; and with even this relatively small amount of proficiency, you are able to get along remarkably well in your new language.

Intermediate Level

The second, intermediate level is attained with approximately 100 to 500 hours of instructional time, depending on the language. At this point you are able to survive without difficulty in a foreign country by conversing in simple terms. You are able to talk about the past, present, and future. Your conversation is understood by native speakers who are accustomed to talking with foreigners. When people talk to you, even though you do not know every word, you understand what they are talking about. This is especially true in situations such as ordering meals, asking directions, obtaining a phone number from the operator, buying tickets, and shopping. When you have difficulty understanding detailed information, you are able to figure it out by asking speakers to repeat what they have said. You are able to read simple paragraphs, social notes, introductory and summary paragraphs in newspapers and magazines, and easy stories. When reading, you are able to figure out some fairly complicated sentences by using clues in context. Your writing skills include letters, short compositions, and simple paragraphs.

Advanced Level

The third, advanced level is attained with approximately 500 to 1500 hours of instructional time. You are able to speak the language satisfactorily in most social and work situations, follow the rules of grammar, and use specific vocabulary. You speak fluently, even though at times you may make a mistake in grammar. You are able to listen and understand face-to-face speech spoken at normal speed by native speakers, but you may still need to ask for some repetition and rewording. While reading, you are able to follow main ideas and some minor ideas when you know something about the subject. You are able to read simple materials containing descriptions, such as novels and nonfiction books. At this level, you can write routine social correspondence in simple sentences, using several paragraphs on familiar topics, and are able to join sentences together so that your discourse sounds authentic.[1] (Notes for all chapters of this book begin on page 101.)

After you have reached the advanced level of proficiency, you will no longer be a student. You will have reached your goal of functioning as a speaker of your new language. Nevertheless, you will continue to improve your proficiency by using the language—reading for pleasure or for your work, visiting or living in a country where your language is spoken, listening to the radio, watching television or movies, and speaking.

To become proficient in your new language takes time and a conscious effort to take advantage of all opportunities to use your language. For now, note the steps you will take on your way up the proficiency ladder and look forward to the opportunity you have to learn a new language.

YOUR APTITUDE FOR FOREIGN LANGUAGES

You may have heard it said that foreign languages come easier to some people than to others. This is true only in limited ways. For example, just as some people have larger vocabularies than others in their first language, similar individual differences can be expected in a second language. However, the real aim of foreign language study is to use your new language to make your ideas known and to find out what others are thinking. Anyone can acquire this ability. In fact, most of the world's population use more than one language regularly. People all over the world, from all social and economic levels, learn two, three, or four languages when they need to. For them, just as for you, learning a new language is quite an ordinary accomplishment for which great intellectual ability is not necessary.

The Indians who live along the Vaupés River in South America must be the world's premier language learners. The Vaupés is located in Brazil and Colombia; it flows into the Rio Negro, which in turn flows into the Amazon. Remote from modern civilization, almost every member of these diverse Indian groups knows three or four languages well. Their culture demands that they marry outside of their own language group, so everyone is born into a bilingual home and needs additional languages to search for a spouse. Adolescents actively learn to speak a few languages in addition to the languages of their parents. As these Indians grow older, they continue to perfect their knowledge of all the languages in their repertoire. They do not think that their language ability is anything unusual; in fact, most of them cannot tell you how many languages they know and would be quite surprised that anyone would want to ask.[2]

So you can see that the ability to learn and use new languages is not limited to a chosen few. While you may know someone who has been unsuccessful in learning a new language, this unfortunate result is not due to the person's lack of intelligence, aptitude, or interest. Rather, success in a new language is mostly a result of the proper set of circumstances that allow your built-in language learning ability to operate at its best. This book will help you create those circumstances.

LEARNING AND ACQUIRING A FOREIGN LANGUAGE

Two kinds of activities are involved in most foreign language study experiences. One is a more or less formal type of activity, which includes studying word lists, completing exercises, memorizing dialogues, and reading or talking about the way the new language works. The second activity occurs almost unconsciously when you understand what is said to you or what you read, when you figure out for yourself how the new language works, and when you try to express your own ideas to convey information in the new language. The first activity is called *learning;* the second, to distinguish it from learning, is called *acquisition.*

Formal learning comes easier to some persons than to others. If you are in a class where the instructor makes learning activities an important part of your course, then you will gain practice in these activities and become better at them. Most people expect to do learning exercises, and they gain confidence when they can do them well. A few individuals are totally bored with the puzzle-solving aspects of language learning, such as conjugating verbs and filling in blanks in exercises. They realize that if they lived in Mexico for twenty years, they would probably never be asked to conjugate a verb or change a sentence from the present to the past tense. Experiencing difficulty in doing such tasks does not mean that ultimately you will not be able to use the new language as successfully as those who find it easier to conjugate verbs and fill in blanks. *The real* objective of foreign language study is to understand and exchange ideas in your new language.

Acquisition, your ultimate goal, takes place almost by itself as you use your new language. You just have to make sure that the samples of the new language which you hear, read, and use are meaningful to you. Suppose you tuned in to Radio Peking in Chinese for one hour a day for a year. Chances are good that at the end of a year you wouldn't understand any more Chinese than you do now, because you wouldn't have had the slightest idea what the speakers were saying. You can't make progress without understanding the meaning.

MAKING PROGRESS IN YOUR NEW LANGUAGE

At first, when you hardly know any words, your conversation will be limited. Most likely, you will use body language and pantomime in order to understand and converse. You will engage in simple conversations about yourself and the people and things around you, read about subjects that are of interest to you and in which you have some background, and play games that help you have fun as you learn your new language. If the selection of language you hear or read contains a few words or expressions that are new to you, so much the better. You acquire the new items because the rest of the context is familiar, and you are able to figure out the new parts. That's how you make progress.

If you do not understand a great deal of what is going on in the language class, it is your responsibility to interrupt and ask for an explanation or clarification. Don't sit back and expect things to become clear later. They might, but then again they might not. You shouldn't take that chance. Since comprehension is a prerequisite to progress in your new language, make certain you understand what is said in your class. As you will discover in the chapter on understanding and speaking, this does not mean that you have to understand every word.

The person who will provide most of the language samples that can help you acquire your new language is your instructor, who knows you personally and is aware of your stage of progress. Your instructor can assess your learning level and communicate with you on that level much better than a textbook or recorded materials. This is the crucial reason why you should attend all of your classes. There are also many things you can do for yourself, outside the structure of a class, that will help with both learning and acquisition. Suggestions and hints for helping yourself are presented throughout this book.

WHERE TO FIND THE RIGHT CLASS FOR YOU

Many organizations offer the opportunity to study a foreign language. These include public school evening classes, private language schools, colleges, correspondence schools, government language schools, and home study agencies that use books, tapes, and computer programs. Some organizations offer total immersion in a foreign language in a school setting or in a foreign country. Which of these is best for you? This depends upon your ultimate goal and your time and financial commitments. Shop around for the foreign language program that is right for you. If you need a reading knowledge of a language, choose a program that stresses reading. If you want to gain oral fluency, choose a program that stresses oral practice. And if you want a crash tourist's course, choose one that is of proven benefit.

The first few days in a foreign language class are crucial to your future success. Assess the course content and the levels of language ability of your classmates. For example, when Mary Ann began Portuguese, she found herself in a class with two students who had lived in Portugal and ten students who were from homes where Portuguese was spoken. Most members of the class were years ahead of her and she felt stupid and defeated from the beginning. She wisely transferred to another class. Don't place yourself in "no win" situations. During the initial class meetings, assess whether the instructor will be teaching at your level of knowledge and whether you will be able to understand the level of conversation.

If you are going to renew the study of a language you began in the past, even years ago, it is important not to assume that because you have been away from the language for some time you need to start at the very beginning. It is just as bad to be in a class that is below your level as it is to be in one that is too advanced. In addition, your knowledge, however small, may demoralize your classmates. At the same time, you may become bored when you realize you are not acquiring much more of the language than you already know. Or worse, you may find at first that the class requires no effort; and when the class suddenly catches up to your level, you may have a hard time becoming involved in the activities. Make sure at the start that you are in the best possible class for your needs and language level. If placement tests or interviews are available, take advantage of them. After a few sessions of your class, ask for the instructor's opinion about whether you are at the right level.

SHOPPING FOR YOUR CLASS

Shopping for the right class is time well spent. As with any kind of purchase, you must know where to look first. After all, you don't go to a hardware store to shop for jogging shoes. The following places are good starting points for finding your foreign language class.

Usually, public school evening classes are taught by competent teachers who understand the needs of beginning students. These classes have minimal fees or are sometimes free to community residents. Foreign language laboratories are usually well equipped and students receive basic knowledge in a carefully structured setting. If you have never studied a foreign language before, this kind of program may give you the structure and security you need. Call the extension or night school division of your local school system for information.

Private language schools cater to the needs of individuals, businesses, industries, and government. Many have day as well as evening classes, and some include total immersion courses of high quality. Private organizations are more expensive, but their classes are smaller and offer more opportunity for individual participation and attention. Look in the telephone directory and then check with your Better Business Bureau for the quality of schools in your area.

Colleges provide long-term structured courses that allow you to move from level to level with ease. If you intend to become a long-term student, you will find these courses valuable because of their sequential structure and the opportunity to learn a language in depth.

Correspondence courses and home study may be arranged through private and public agencies. Some universities offer excellent correspondence courses that are accredited by the universities' regional accrediting associations. College credit may often be obtained. If you wish to receive credit toward a university degree for your home study course, contact your university before enrolling to find out its limitations on correspondence study credits. Lessons from these schools are usually evaluated promptly, and the student may also be graded orally by using tapes. Private agencies may be accredited by the National Home Study Council. Advertisements for home study should always be checked out with the Better Business Bureau.

Many people study a language using tapes and books obtained at a public library or purchased in a bookstore. After your initial interest in the materials has been satisfied, you need a strong personal commitment in order to keep studying. Few people study beyond the first few tapes or units of work. Individual study requires strong, personal discipline and a commitment that few people have. However, tapes, cassettes, and books used in home study are good starting points for beginning learners and also contain good supplemental materials for all learners. But be wary of claims made in advertisements, and be aware of the limitations of home and individual study in the learning of a foreign language.

If you are being prepared for service overseas by a government or private agency, you may be fortunate to be placed in a three- to six-month total immersion program in which your spouse and children are included. These programs are usually of high quality and you will be lucky to participate. Also, they are ideal if you wish to learn a language efficiently and quickly. The ideas in this book should help you to gain confidence in your ability to participate in such a program.

KNOW YOUR ATTITUDES

Foreign language study can seem frightening to you if you have heard that only persons with a special linguistic gift are able to learn a new language. Every person in the world learns to speak at least one language, so we know that every human being has the gift of language ability. Second language learners may be gifted or dull, but a second or even a third language is possible for most people. Certainly young children learn a language with less accent and more ease than teens or adults, but remember that many oldsters learn second languages, too. Take Jay Sommer, named national Teacher of the Year in 1981-82, who teaches foreign languages in New York. He spent his early teens in a Nazi concentration camp and in the Russian army. When he escaped to Italy, he learned Italian by talking to people, singing their songs, and reading the literature of their great writers. When he came to America, he learned English in a short time in a New York City public school. By absorbing the culture and the ideas of each language, he was able to learn a second and a third language. You can do the same!

When studying a foreign language, you place yourself in an environment in which your learned behaviors of communication are of little value. At times you will be at a loss and not know what to do. You may even feel stupid. Do not despair when you are in such a situation! Pretend you are in a foreign country. What would you do to communicate with others? Follow the guidelines in this book and you *will learn* to communicate in your new language. At first you may feel awkward and foolish when you hear yourself saying new sounds. Don't give up, and don't be afraid to make mistakes. Laugh at your mistakes, and keep talking and listening to yourself and to others.

Notice the attitudes of your classmates. In almost every foreign language class there is a "shy Jane." She is afraid to seem foolish, so she blushes and swallows her words when it is time to speak. "Loud-mouthed Joe" learns a few words and tries to answer all questions with the few phrases he knows, plus a lot of wisecracks. "I'll-try-anything Pete" keeps on trying and laughing at his mistakes. He doesn't critize himself for making mistakes. He asks the teacher for repetition and clarification. You know he will learn the language because of his attitude, but Jane and Joe will need to change their attitudes if they are to succeed.

What should you do? Walk into your foreign language class with a positive attitude. Decide that you will be successful. Begin to speak in your new language as soon as you feel ready, and enjoy trying to say new sounds and words. While speaking, do not think too much about rules of pronunciation and grammar. Let your voice flow freely; listen carefully and blend your voice with the sounds of the language. Don't worry about the differences between your new language and your mother tongue. Allow your voice to take precedence over the rules. Practice your new skills constantly, in and out of class, with anyone who will talk to you. Believe you will succeed and you will!

You may consider taking a language aptitude test at a school or college. Understand that these tests are only successful in predicting your ability at *formal tasks,* such as analysis and list memorization, which are sometimes associated with learning in a foreign language class. These tests do not take into consideration personal drive and perseverance or your ability to learn in less formal settings. Your *attitude,* not your aptitude, can make all the difference in your chances for success.

Be realistic. It takes time to learn a new language. Remember how long it took you to be truly proficient in your native language. Set realistic goals and objectives. Do not expect to be able to understand television shows and to speak like a native in one or two years. Take your time.

TIME, TIME, TIME

Let's suppose that you have found the foreign language program you want and you are ready to begin. Now you need to plan your time wisely. How much time will you need for studying? How can you decide whether the time you need is available? Making a weekly time management plan will help you to plan for your study, class, and commuting schedules. A time management plan, like the sample shown here, will serve as a reminder to you of what you wish to accomplish. We are creatures of habit, and habits, once established, are difficult to break. Of course, this can be to your advantage, as well. Habits save time and provide structure. Since you've already decided what you'll do and when, you don't have to consider alternatives. Crossing off completed tasks on your time management plan helps you feel good and is a stimulus for following through with the remainder of your tasks.

Time Management Plan

MONDAY

Hours	Activity
6	Breakfast
7	Shower, dress, etc.
8	Commute
9	↓
10	Work
11	↓
12	Lunch/Flextime
1	↓
2	↓
3	Work
4	↓
5	Commute
6	Dinner/Family time
7	Commute/Class
8	Class/Commute
9	Flextime
10	Study

Notes

Study: Review class work
         Read Chapter 6

To do in Flextime

1. pay bills
2. telephone Harry
3. make doctor's appt.

You'll be in trouble from the start if you lack sufficient time to accomplish your goal. How will you determine whether or not you have the time you need? On paper, plot out a preliminary weekly time management plan before you sign up for a particular course so that you will be sure you have enough time for your studies. You'll find that a weekly time management plan is an important decision-making tool.

PREPARING YOUR TIME MANAGEMENT PLAN

At first, developing a plan may seem cumbersome and time-consuming; nevertheless, you should stay with it. You will realize the advantages of a time management plan when you've worked with the idea for a while. Here is what you should do. Fold seven sheets of lined 8½ " × 11 " white or colored paper in half lengthwise. Use colored paper, if possible, to distinguish these papers from your other papers. Write one day of the week at the top of each sheet. In the margin, write numbers in a column to represent the hours of the day. Begin with the hour you get up in the morning and end with the hour you go to bed. Each space will stand for one hour of your day.

On a separate piece of paper, list your major activities during each day. Don't list an activity you've decided to give up in order to study your new language. List class hours and an estimate of study times. How many hours should you set aside for the study of your language? Use this rule of thumb: note how many hours you will spend in class and multiply those hours by the difficulty level of the subject. If language learning comes easily to you, the difficulty level is *2;* if it isn't easy but it is not very difficult, the level for you is *3.* If you expect studying is going to be a struggle, the level is *4.* Multiplying the number of hours spent in class by the difficulty level equals your study time for the week. For example, if you spend three hours in class each week, and the difficulty level is *4,* then twelve hours of study is what you need per week. Remember, this is only an estimate; twelve hours may be too many or too few. But until you really know the amount of study time you need, this formula will provide a reasonable guideline for success.

Now you're ready to use your seven time sheets to list your activities. Use a pencil, as you may need to make changes. Do not block in study hours yet. For each day, block in one hour during the day and one during the evening, and label these hours ''Flextime.'' Leave time for the unexpected and for the activities you know are part of your life but don't always happen regularly. Flextime will help you accommodate these activities.

''Clumping'' is a technique to save you from writing too much. If you prepare breakfast, feed the children, wash dishes, shower, and get dressed between 6:00 and 8:00 a.m., then clump these activities under one heading. Be specific in labeling; later you will develop your own streamlined coding system. When you've finished block-ing in your activities (except for study time), place all seven sheets in front of you so you can see them at one glance. Count the number of empty time blocks. These blocks represent the hours you have avail-able for study.

The study techniques in this book can help you reduce the num-ber of hours you need to study. However, you cannot do well in your new language unless you have the time to study. Follow the rule of thumb for estimating the number of study hours you will need. If, after blocking out your activities, you find you have too few hours for study, you'll need to make some decisions. What activities are you willing to give up in order to free blocks of time for study? You may need to weigh and compare the importance of your choices. Is the language course worth an hour-long commute? Should you se-lect a language course taught closer to your home? Put your activi-ties in order of priority and adjust your schedule accordingly. When this is done, you may take the course with confidence because you know you have the time to study. Each week, plot out a time man-agement plan, and carry your daily plan with you as a reminder of your commitments.

SUMMARY

You have chosen your goals, assessed your commitment to the study of a new language, and set up a time management plan. You have also considered that your *aptitude* for foreign languages is far less crucial to your success than your *attitude*. Now you are ready to begin your study of a foreign language. You are on your way to success!

The next step is to incorporate your new language more fully into your lifestyle. Chapter 2 suggests ways to use your new language in daily living and to make it an integral part of your life. When your new language becomes part of your life, your listening, speaking, reading, and writing abilities improve, and you will use the lan-guage in practical ways that are personally meaningful to you.

2

Incorporating a New Language into Your Lifestyle

Language study is not something you do only during class and study times. Learning a new language means using it in and out of the classroom. It means thinking, speaking, listening, and reading in your new language whenever you can. Your language needs to become a useful and valued part of your daily life. Think of the ways you hope to use your new language in the future. If you wish to keep up to date with events in a foreign country, buy that country's newspapers and begin reading headlines. If you are interested in contemporary music, listen to a foreign language radio station. In this way, your new language becomes part of your life as you use it to meet the goals of your personal study.

When you study a language in a formal structure, such as a class or a correspondence course, each day's work builds on what was learned the day before. For example, on Tuesday you may be writing about cooking. However, you will be unable to do this unless you have done Monday's assignment, which was to learn the names of various kinds of foods. In foreign language study, each lesson and each assignment should be completed promptly, or you may be unable to continue with the next assignment. This means that you need to develop daily and weekly time management plans and follow them faithfully. If you have a full-time job, faithfulness to your time management plans may prove difficult. However, it is possible to hold a job and learn a new language at the same time. Here's how you can do it.

WORK ALL DAY AND STUDY, TOO

How do you find time for study? First, look at your time management plan. You may find you still do not have enough time to study; in this case, revise your plan. What activities can you eliminate? What activities must be retained? If you still do not have enough time, you should know that a language is one subject you can study while you are showering, dressing, eating, exercising, or going to work. These are good times to review what you have memorized or to see how many of the objects within your view you can name in your new language. Tape your class meetings or record yourself reading aloud; then listen to the cassettes while you drive or, with earphones, listen while you wait at a doctor's office or at the bank.

If you still do not have time for studying, try to eliminate social or household duties that others could do for you. Do you really need to chair the community rummage sale? Learn to say "no" politely to requests that are not in your best interest, and learn to delegate work to others. Keep in mind that you don't have time for new, as well as old, activities.

If you need to find still more time to study, organize routine tasks more efficiently, especially those related to eating, grooming, and cleaning. Your home and work place need to be tidy enough to find anything you want quickly, but you should not spend a long time keeping everything perfect when you need time to study. The time you save may give you a few more minutes with your new language.

As you make time for your new language, do not eliminate all recreational activities from your life. Your body and your mind need some vigorous activity every day. You will find that you learn better and your mind is more alert when physical activities are part of your daily plans.

Because memorization is an important part of language study, your time management plan should include definite times to work on memorization. Chapter 3 tells you what you can do during these sessions, but here is an example of one person's memorization plan:

> Miriam wrote the most important words she wanted to learn on cards, and she carried them in her coat pocket so that she could use spare moments for memorizing. She first reviewed the words ten minutes after writing the cards because she knew research has shown

that the best time to review is just ten minutes after initial learning. She followed this with a review sixty minutes later. She then spaced her memorization reviews every twenty-four hours after that until the words were permanent in her memory.

This scheme works because information recently learned is in your temporary, nonpermanent memory and must be reviewed at specific intervals in order to become permanent.

Each individual has times during the day when the mind is clear and alert for study. Some people study best at night; others in the morning. If you are able to practice your new language during your best hours, your learning will be more efficient. However, if you work, you may have to study during your less efficient hours. If this is so, take a few minutes after a busy day to renew your energy and clear your mind. Some people take a short nap, some jog, some eat a snack or dinner, and some talk to friends. You will find that a few minutes of relaxation will renew your vigor, and you will be ready to think in your new language with a clear, alert mind.

USING WHAT YOU KNOW

Because you are already fluent in at least one language, you have much linguistic knowledge upon which to build. This knowledge helps you make more efficient use of your time because you incorporate previous knowledge into the new. You learn by associating new knowledge with familiar ideas and then forging links between the two. Look for the linkages between your two languages. Are the sentence structures the same? Which elements are different? Which words are similar in spelling? Are their meanings and uses also similar? When you first encounter your new language, look for words that are similar to those you already know, and you will find that you have a surprisingly good vocabulary in your new language.

The next several chapters provide ways to capitalize on your present knowledge in learning a new language. Here is an example. A German-language advertisement for a resort on the Mediterranean contains the following words: *Bungalows, Restaurant, Tennis, Yoga, Swimming-pool, Nightclub, Schnorcheln,* and *Stereokonzerte.* The meaning of the last two words can be surmised on the basis of similarity to

English. Add to this just the tiniest amount of knowledge of German, and you will have no trouble knowing what goes on at this resort.

ADAPTING YOUR ATTITUDES

As you begin to learn a new language, you are also beginning the adventure of adapting to an exciting new culture in which the ordinary things you learned to do as a child may be completely out of place. Perhaps you were taught to sit up straight, never place your elbows on the table while eating, and to take small bites of food. Then you decide to learn the language of a society in which good table manners include elbows on the table and the slurping of large amounts of food. How would you react if you were in the country and were invited to dinner? Would you make the experience an enjoyable adventure, or would you pull back into a "my culture is best" attitude? Language learning is the development of reading and speaking abilities based on an accurate knowledge of the culture. If you are to become successful at functioning in the culture of your new language, you need to be flexible in your thinking, possibly adjusting your attitudes.

Because each language is based in a unique cultural milieu, whatever is written or said in each language is grounded in the social, moral, and religious beliefs of its people. As a learner, you need to know what these people believe about such things as individual freedom, rights of children, home life, the future of the world, and life after death. Without this knowledge, you may miss meanings in oral and written discourse. Therefore, you should take every opportunity to absorb the cultural knowledge that is available to you through friendships, films, and books. Seek out speakers of your new language and place yourself in situations that enable you to see and hear your new language used in natural ways.

As you begin to talk to people in your new language, you may be surprised to discover that your intended meaning is not conveyed to the listener because you have not used the expected *body language*. The new language you are learning is not just communication with words. It is also knowing how to look at another person and knowing which gestures and which tone of voice to use. In North America, when we talk to others, we look into their eyes; in many cultures this is not appropriate behavior, especially when speaking to those who are older or of higher social standing. Eye, head, finger, and shoulder movements vary from culture to culture, as do facial expressions. If you understand body language, you may be able to understand a conversation even though you do not know all or even most of the words. Body language is learned by observing native speakers and by copying their gestures. Practicing in front of a mirror will help you develop these needed skills.

Language learning also involves understanding that words and phrases may have different meanings, depending on the situation or the people taking part in the conversation. Certain words connote friendliness, respect, or social and economic equality; these must be used in the appropriate social settings. In your own language you have learned to say things in different ways in different situations, as in the following example:

> When James greets his son in the morning, he may say "Hi, my big man!" His wife is greeted with "Morning, Honey." Neither of these greetings would be appropriate for his boss; James may extend to him a formal "Good morning, sir." James might not want to order his secretary to open the window, but by asking, "Isn't it hot in here?" he can get the window opened without issuing a direct command.

In your new language, knowledge of this sort should be a part of your studies. You should expect instructors and materials to provide appropriate phrases for use in different social settings.

Learning the words and rules of a new language—in addition to studying the people, culture, and body language—may seem like a lot to tackle. But you don't have to learn everything overnight. Nor do you have to learn everything formally. There are many ways to increase your knowledge and have fun in the bargain. For example, you can make your new language an enjoyable part of your life by doing some of the following activities:

1. Read newspapers and magazines in the language.

2. Learn songs and poems in the language.

3. Listen to radio stations and watch TV programs.

4. Go to dinner at a restaurant where food from the culture is served.

5. Go to films or attend foreign language film festivals.

6. Take a part-time job or volunteer your services in a setting where you must speak the language.

7. Attend services at a place of worship where the language is spoken.

8. Write to a pen pal.

9. Spend a year, a semester, a summer, or a vacation in a country where your new language is spoken.

10. Become a host for students from a country where the language is spoken. (Youth organizations are always looking for responsive and responsible host families.)

THINKING IN YOUR NEW LANGUAGE

Incorporating a new language into your lifestyle entails learning to think in your new language without translating between your new language and your native language. Translating is time-consuming, and you will use your new language more efficiently if you avoid trying to figure out how every single idea would be expressed in both languages. In your native language you talk to yourself all the time; begin to do this in your new language.

As you walk to the bus stop in the morning, name the things you see. When you shop at the supermarket, name the items you buy. Silently practice social communication skills. Pretend you are meeting an important person. What would you say? How would the person reply? Include appropriate gestures, and practice until the ''conversation'' runs smoothly.

With a friend or classmate, role-play practical situations. Here are a few suggestions:

1. You have been taken to a hospital after an accident. State what is wrong. Ask to go to the bathroom or to find a telephone. Ask about the details of your treatment.

2. You are in jail for reckless driving. Ask for a lawyer; ask to contact your embassy and your family.

3. You are lost on a city street or in the countryside. Ask how to return to a familiar place. Or assume that someone is lost in your hometown; give the person directions to a central point.

4. Your car has broken down; ask about towing and repairs.

5. You are traveling by train, bus, subway, or airplane. Ask about fares and destinations.

6. You want to buy an item in a store. Try to calculate quickly if the item is a bargain in U.S. dollars.

7. You have received change after paying for a meal. You think that the amount of change is incorrect.

8. You are in a hotel and have the key to your room, but no one at the front desk will help you find your room.

9. You are hungry while traveling and want to buy food.

REGULATING STUDY TIME

Learn to regulate and control your environment when you study and practice. Choose a quiet time and find a place where distractions are few. Train your family and friends to be considerate of your right to study effectively. Shut yourself off from others: close the door, turn off the TV and radio, take your phone off the hook, or hang a ''do not disturb'' sign on the door. For example, Ginger chose her two-year-old son's nap time as her study time. She closed her door to neighbors and took the telephone off the hook. This was her time to study, and she used it wisely.

When you study, monitor yourself. Are you really using your new language, or are you daydreaming, doodling, and studying in unproductive ways? As you begin to work, make a list of what you intend to accomplish. Give yourself an amount of time for each item. With your eye on the clock, see whether your time schedule is realistic. Check each item off your list as it is completed. This will help you set small objectives and give you a sense of accomplishment when each portion of your study time is finished.

SUMMARY

This chapter has shown that you can combine study with a full-time job by developing efficient time management plans. You have also seen how to use your linguistic knowledge to enhance the acquisition of your new language, adapt your attitudes to new cultures, think in your new language, and regulate your study time.

Because memorization is the key to efficient language learning, the next chapter is perhaps the most important chapter in this book. In it, you will discover ideas and techniques that will help you memorize efficiently. Included are sections on how to develop your long-term memory, learn in meaningful wholes, memorize vocabulary, and prepare for exams.

3

You Can
Memorize

The ability to memorize is the most needed skill in learning a new language. Nearly everything you study, including vocabulary and rules of grammar, will be memorized. As you begin the study of your new language, do not be overwhelmed by the amount of memorization required. Instead, make plans to learn a few words or phrases each day, and you will be surprised by how much you have memorized in a week or a month. This chapter will present a variety of ways to memorize efficiently. Choose techniques you believe will work for you, prepare time management plans that make sense in terms of the time and effort you are able to expend, and begin your memorization plan with confidence that you will learn to memorize well.

SHORT-TERM AND LONG-TERM MEMORY

Research about memory has shown that there are three sequential phases of memorization: pre-short-term memory (pre-STM), short-term memory (STM), and long-term memory (LTM). In pre-STM, information stays with you for less than a minute, and no conscious effort is made to retain the information. In STM, information lasts longer than in pre-STM, requires conscious effort to remember, and is lost from your memory if not reviewed. In LTM, however, information may last for a lifetime. It should be obvious, then, that *the goal of memorization is to enter information into your long-term memory.*

The following discussion will describe the steps in memorization from pre-STM to STM and finally to LTM. The examples are related to the memorization of vocabulary, but you may use the same steps for any memorization. New vocabulary items enter your memory through pre-STM and STM, but unless they reach LTM, they will not be available to you when you need them. "The Path to Long-term Memory and Recall" chart summarizes the steps through which vocabulary is learned, retained, and recalled.

The Path to Long-term Memory and Recall

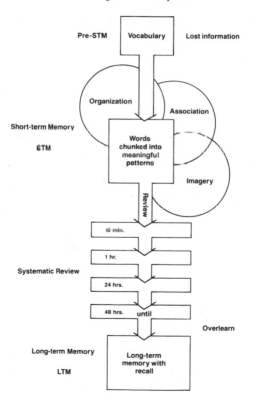

At the pre-STM stage, you are aware of new vocabulary through listening and reading; but if you wish to use a new word, it must at least reach STM, or it will be lost. You have experienced this information loss many times. For example, you may have read a number in the telephone book and recalled it just long enough to dial the number once. If your call was not completed, you may have had to look up the number again because it had never entered your memory. It should be obvious that pre-STM is not useful in language learning. You must place new vocabulary in STM, and then in LTM.

TECHNIQUES FOR MEMORIZATION

In STM, you retain vocabulary by using techniques known as chunking, association, imagery, and organization. Here is a story that illustrates the process of "chunking" words by association and organization.

Rachel and Robert were visiting friends who spoke Spanish. Rachel became very frustrated when a number of people with Spanish names were introduced to her. She wondered how she could remember so many new names: Maria, Sofía, Enrique, Carlos, Hildebrando, Juan, Pedro, Marcos, Carmelita, and Elena. Robert, on the other hand, seemed to learn the names quickly. Rachel's mind felt like a sieve with names pouring through and disappearing into nowhere. Later, she asked Robert how he remembered the names so well. "All those names disappeared from my memory as soon as I heard them," said Rachel.

Robert explained that he associated the names in smaller chunks. "I separated the four children's names from the adults' names," said Robert. "The children were Juan, Sofía, Elena, and Carlos. I thought of a sentenced based on the first letter of each name: '*J*ust *S*ee *E*ach *C*hild.' Then, I repeated the sentence and the names two or three times until I could remember them."

"How did you remember the names of the adults?" asked Rachel.

"Those were more difficult," said Robert. "I remembered them by the first letters of their names and by association. I tried to organize the names in a way that would help me remember. One name began with *C,* one with *E,* one *H,* one *M;* and two were biblical names, Pedro and Marcos. The adults' names were Carlos, Enrique, Hildebrando, María, Pedro, and Marcos."

You can experiment with these techniques as you memorize. Association and chunking can help you organize vocabulary items into meaningful groups and at least help you enter them into your short-term memory.

"The Path to Long-term Memory and Recall" chart indicates that the use of imagery aids memorization. For example, in order to memorize the word for "flower" in your new language, visualize a flower; then visualize the word for "flower" written on a label. Next, see yourself attaching the label to the flower you are imaging. Then stand back and visualize what you have done. Try for the sharpest image possible, but don't become anxious if this proves difficult. You will develop skill as you practice.

To develop your mental powers of imagery together with association, think of words you might associate with flowers, such as *garden, pretty,* and *vase.* Visualize these words surrounding the word *flower.* In your imagination, attach labels to these items as you did for the flower, and visualize this chunk of ideas with the sharpest image possible. You will find that chunking similar ideas together and visualizing is a good way to help yourself remember.

It is not a good idea to try to memorize lists of words in isolation because recall may be very difficult or impossible. The same plan used to learn or store information in your memory is used to recall it. If words are to be stored permanently in your memory and recalled later, they need to be stored in an orderly fashion and associated with a network of ideas. A list of unconnected words is difficult to recall because it is not associated with a network of ideas. Therefore, in initial stages of memorization, develop networks of ideas and group items into an organization that is meaningful to you.

STM is your first step in memorization, but this initial step must be followed by systematic review until your vocabulary is overlearned and reaches your LTM. Otherwise, you will have wasted your time at the STM step because the fruits of your efforts are likely to be forgotten. Many learners conscientiously learn vocabulary at the STM stage, but they do not take the next steps in the memorization sequence. Then they wonder why recall is difficult. Recall depends on three factors: (1) associating ideas in meaningful chunks; (2) reviewing by using the associations developed in STM; and (3) overlearning until recall is automatic.

Newly memorized vocabulary should be reviewed ten minutes after initial learning, sixty minutes after that, and again twenty-four hours later. You should then review about every two days until recall is automatic. Automatic recall is your memory goal; keep reviewing until you reach it.

If you are unable to recall vocabulary on demand, reassess your study habits. You may not have reviewed consistently or long enough, or your initial steps in STM may not have been associated with familiar knowledge and chunked in ways that were meaningful to you. You may need to go back and study some vocabulary items again, using different associations and images. Keep developing your techniques until you are able to memorize efficiently.

GOALS AND PLANS

Set definite memory goals and study plans. Discover how many words you are able to learn comfortably each day or week; then raise your expectations a little. Don't allow yourself to become frustrated or discouraged. If you are using your spare time to work on your new language, go easy on yourself. Only make demands upon yourself when you have the energy and time to fulfill them. But do not be too gentle. Learn new vocabulary every day. Don't limit yourself to the vocabulary contained in your course work; later you will be rewarded in unexpected ways for your extra knowledge. Whatever you would like to talk about in your new language, learn the appropriate vocabulary on your own. For example, find out the names of the major rivers in the area where your language is spoken, or the names of items of clothing, or the pet names people use for their children. This is the kind of goal that causes you to stretch your mind without discouraging or frustrating you.

If you have too much to memorize, take longer to complete a course. If you are taking a college course, audit for a semester, and then take the course for credit when you feel comfortable with the amount of work.

When planning your study, memorize in time blocks that are best for you; this could mean ten, thirty, or sixty minutes. Take five-minute breaks during your memorization, but guard against giving yourself longer breaks. If possible, plan your study so that you memorize when your energy level is high, and do easier types of study when your energy level is low.

SQ3R

You may find that the well-known study technique called SQ3R (Survey, Question, Read, Review, and Recite) will help you plan what to do when you study. This technique is especially helpful if information is in narrative form and you must remember not only vocabulary but also major and minor ideas. It is particularly useful for learning vocabulary that is presented in context rather than in the form of a list.

First, *survey* the new information. How is it organized? Do the headings and subheadings of the narrative give you memory clues? What are the main ideas and important vocabulary?

Question as you read, asking yourself the following: What vocabulary items and other information are worth remembering? What do I know already? In what ways could I organize the information in order to remember it efficiently?

Read the major ideas first. Circle important vocabulary and think about what these items mean in context. Skim information of lesser importance. Organize information and new vocabulary into chunks of ideas and concepts. As you read, begin to work on placing items into your STM.

Review the information, answer the questions you formulated, and restate the major concepts and ideas.

Recite aloud the major and minor ideas and vocabulary you have memorized; speaking aloud is especially important in a foreign language. Relearn the items you cannot remember. Check the accuracy of your memorization by writing from memory and comparing your notes with the original source.

HOW TO MEMORIZE

Here are the ideas you have been waiting for, the techniques and tricks for memorization! You can use these techniques for review as well as for initial memorization. Some of the techniques will be more useful to you than others, and some will help you with certain memorization problems more than with others.

Memorization is not just a bag of tricks; it is the application of theories about how people learn to memorize. In order to memorize, you need to use goal-setting and time management plans as well as sensible memorization techniques. You need to find the techniques that work most effectively for you and for your particular goals. For example, one of the authors of this book once memorized 2500 German words in ten days in order to pass a graduate reading exam; however, a month later few of the words could be recalled, since they had been placed in STM and not in LTM.

Would you like to know how 2500 words were memorized quickly? The words were divided into ten groups of 250 related or similar items. Each group of 250 was subdivided into ten groups of 25. Each day was then divided into twelve study hours. During each hour, 25 words were memorized by visualizing, reciting, and writing words and meanings. For the last ten minutes of each hour, all words from the previous hour were reviewed. Every five hours, all words from the previous five hours were reviewed. Just before going to sleep each night, all words for the day, plus the words from the previous day, were reviewed.

Before the learner got out of bed in the morning, all words were reviewed once. Each morning it was necessary to awaken thirty to forty-five minutes earlier in order to review the growing number of words. If you experiment with this method, you will not sleep much, but you will find your mind working clearly and in organized ways; and the sheer exhilaration of the process will motivate you to keep going until your goal is reached. However, full-time memorization for more than a few days is not recommended. The main thing you should notice about this technique is that it emphasizes review before and after sleeping.

Other popular techniques include mnemonics, concept trees, chunking, visualization, association, dramatics, modalities, and guessing. Yes, guessing—it is an efficient technique if not overused. Since visualization and association have already been discussed, the next sections will explain the other techniques.

MNEMONICS

Mnemosyne was the goddess of memory in Greek mythology. Mnemonic techniques are those intended to assist memory and are usually related to the association of new ideas with old. For example, a list of words that rhyme may be easier to remember than a nonrhyming list. Words related to a story or to a topic, or joined to some known idea, are remembered much more easily than isolated words or words in unrelated lists. When you are trying to learn new vocabulary, associate the new words with known words. Some mnemonic ideas you could try follow.

Relate Words in Groups

Related words are easier to memorize than unrelated words, so learn words in related groups.

Furniture	Fruit
chair	apple
table	orange
bed	peach
cabinet	pear

This means that even though your assignment may involve learning the names of four kinds of fruit, with little extra effort you could learn several more kinds on your own once you started thinking about fruit.

Group Words by Use

Group words that could be associated according to the kind of situation in which they could be used.

Prepositions

up	down
left	right
above	below
in front of	behind
next to	

Relate the Unrelated

Invent a meaningful sentence or acronym that lets you group items that are actually unrelated.

"*Just See Each Child*" represents Juan, Sofia, Elena, and Carlos.
"BECAUSE" represents *best, ever, cat, animal, up, some,* and *easy.*

Group Words in Categories

Learn words in categories; for example, think of all the compliments and insults you could make about someone.

CONCEPT TREES

A concept tree is developed around a concept that is meaningful to you. It is used to group similar ideas by associating known ideas with new ideas through the use of a drawing. Begin by placing a key vocabulary word in the center of a page. Write or draw related words around it in ways that make sense to you. In the examples, the concept "hair" is used.

A Concept Tree Using Related Words

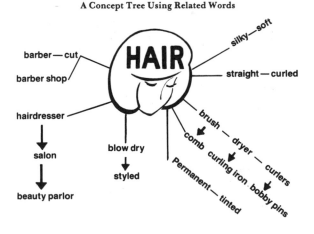

A Concept Tree Using Drawings

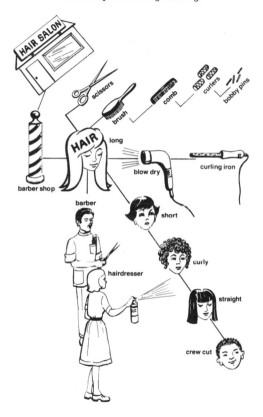

Notice that some concepts can be more easily understood using drawings, and some using words. For example, ''silky'' and ''soft'' are not easy to draw. Many learners use concept trees as the central core of their memorization plan, and you may find this technique to be a solution to your memorization problems as well.

CHUNKING

Chunking the words you want to learn into groups that are meaningful to you reduces the number of items you learn individually. If you are learning adjectives, learn their opposites at the same time, whether or not they are part of the assignment. If you are memorizing any word, look around for similar meanings to include at the same time. For example, while learning *yesterday,* learn how to say *last week, last month, last year,* and *ago;* perhaps add *tomorrow, next week,* and *next year.* Attach the ideas of your chunks together to form larger units of thought, and you will find that larger units are easier to memorize than smaller ones.

DRAMATICS, BODY LANGUAGE, AND PANTOMIME

The use of dramatics, body language, and pantomime aids memory because you tend to remember what you have experienced. For example, if you want to remember *laugh, cry, weep, smile,* and *grin,* write the words on cards and place them in front of a mirror. First say each word and pantomime the action. Then make up sentences or stories using all the words and dramatize the sentences or stories.

MODALITIES

When you memorize, use your best learning modality—visual, tactile, or audio. Many people remember things better if they have seen them. If your best modality is visual, read and reread the vocabulary you are learning. Look at the spelling carefully. Close your eyes and visualize the words, or write them from memory, until you can do it easily. If the new word is *steal,* visualize a bank holdup. Draw pictures to illustrate words. Memorize in front of a mirror, using appropriate gestures and body language. During initial study, make certain that your mind has taken an accurate picture of both word and meaning. Write new words from memory and check for accuracy. Carry a notebook with the words written in concept trees and look at your new words in spare moments. All these activities provide visual contact with your new language.

If your best modality is tactile, write new words and their meanings from memory until you can write them easily. At first, copy from a written source; then try to write from memory.

If you remember things best when you have heard them, repeat the words aloud, and then spell them aloud, until you can say them easily. Record your new vocabulary items, with their meanings, on tape three or four times. Listen to your tape while driving to work or doing household tasks. Be sure to find time to test your memory by repeating new words from memory. Use each new word in a sentence or story, and say it aloud; you will be reviewing old vocabulary at the same time. Some people find that rhythmically clapping for each syllable while reciting aloud is a help to their memory.

Perhaps you memorize best using a combination of modalities. Find out what works best, and combine the techniques just described.

GUESSING

Guessing is an effective method for discovering the meaning of a new word. It is the method you use most in your first language. When you read a new word, you can usually guess its meaning from context. Often, as you continue to read, the meaning of the word is further clarified and you do not need to use a dictionary. Guessing is actually the technique that saves you from expending inordinate amounts of time and effort using the other techniques. Your comprehension of new words is likely to be as accurate as a result of guessing as it would have been if you had used a dictionary.

A SAMPLE PROBLEM

Now that you have seen the major techniques for memorization, let's see how you could use them to memorize a group of words. The following sample shows the use of guessing and association techniques to memorize a list of vegetables in Spanish. The words are as follows:

rábanos	cebollas
espinacas	nabos
maíz	perejil
habas	moniatos
espárragos	lechuga
remolachas	tomates
champiñones	judías verdes
coles	patatas
zanahorias	arroz
guisantes	coliflor

Begin by trying to guess as many meanings as possible. You will notice that some words look like their counterparts in English. You could probably guess these without any other clues:

espinacas (spinach)

tomates (tomatoes)

patatas (potatoes)

espárragos (asparagus)

coliflor (cauliflower)

Other vegetables may have a form you can associate with an English word, or with a word of similar meaning:

rábanos (radishes)	The first two letters of each word are the same.
coles (cabbages)	This associates with *cole slaw.*
lechuga (lettuce)	The first two letters of each word are the same.
maíz (corn)	This associates with *maize.*
perejil (parsley)	The first letter of each word is the same, and both words have seven letters.

The remaining words do not have obvious associations of meaning or form; therefore, you need to create your own associations and make your own connections. Here are suggestions for remembering some of these words:

guisantes (peas)	*Guisantes* sounds like *geese.* Visualize geese eating green peas.
judías verdes (green beans)	*Judías* looks, though it doesn't sound, like *judges.* Visualize judges dressed in long green gowns that look like green beans.
habas (lima beans)	*Habas* has three letters found in *beans: b, a,* and *s.* Visualize lima beans.
cebollas (onions)	*-boll-* looks like *ball.* Visualize a "ball" of onions.
champiñones (mushrooms)	Did you know that mushrooms are "champion" vegetables?
arroz (rice)	*-roz* resembles *rice.*
zanahorias (carrots)	You try these!
nabos (turnips)	
remolachas (beets)	
moniatos (sweet potatoes)	

This plan for memorizing a fairly large list shows that memorizing these words is not difficult. You can do it by guessing and association, and by developing your abilities in the use of the techniques presented in this chapter.

PREPARING FOR EXAMS

If you are enrolled in a formal foreign language course, you will want to use memorization techniques to prepare for tests and examinations. Since foreign language learning is based on daily use of your new language, and since each day's activity builds on the previous day's, cramming for exams is not a sensible idea. However, even if you have not kept up with course work or have not developed daily memorization plans, there are ways to put your memorization techniques to good use before a test.

First, choose the vocabulary you believe you will need for the test. If you are lucky, you will choose words that you can use on the test; even if you are unlucky and memorize words you cannot use this time, you will certainly be able to use them in the future.

Set yourself a time schedule. If you have five hours to study and 75 words to learn, memorize the easiest 20 words or so during the first half hour. Then divide the rest into meaningful categories and learn about 20 an hour. Use the last hour for review. Be sure to take five-minute breaks each hour, and review all words at the end of each hour.

If you go to sleep at this point and awaken early the next morning to review the words, you will most likely remember them until exam time. However, do not go to a movie or watch television before the exam. The ideas from the movie or TV program may interfere with your memorized words, and you may forget some of them. See the movie after the exam.

DEVELOPING YOUR MEMORIZATION SKILLS

To help you further in developing your memorization abilities, here are some excellent ideas, and a summation of the essentials of successful memorization.

1. Choose groups of words that form meaningful categories. Groups of related words are learned more easily because they are associated in meaningful thought units. For example, you might wish to know some Spanish words that you could use when you go to a restaurant. They will be readily learned because they are associated and meaningful to you.

     restaurante (restaurant)

     camarero (waiter)

     mantel (tablecloth)

     cuenta (check)

     propina (tip)

     ⋮

2. Learn easy words first. Identify the easy words and memorize them quickly. Then concentrate your efforts and most of your time on the items you find difficult to remember.

3. Use concept trees that illustrate meaningful categories. Concept trees organize your words into meaningful groups for study and prevent you from studying words that are not associated with one another. Through association, the words in concept trees are learned easily.

4. Organize vocabulary in notebooks, on index cards, or in a word processor. An organizational plan will save you time and effort. Organize concept trees in notebooks; write words with their meanings on numbered, dated, and color-coded cards; or store them in a word processor, adding to each category as you learn more words, and print them out as study aids.

5. Use your most efficient learning modality. Know your best modality or combination of modalities, and experiment with techniques until you find the ones that are most efficient for you.

6. Review and recall by using the same techniques you used during initial memorization. Vocabulary is entered into STM and LTM through your most effective memorization techniques. In order to recall vocabulary from your memory, you should use the same network of ideas you created to remember the words initially. If you do this, you will discover that your vocabulary can be recalled without difficulty.

7. Use your memorized knowledge in practical ways. Recall is aided by using your growing vocabulary in practical situations. Use your new words in conversation and in writing; make them part of your daily life.

8. Review until your vocabulary is in your permanent memory. Your goal in memorization is the placement of vocabulary in LTM for instant recall. This means reviewing regularly until you are able to recall each word at will. Some words are easier to learn than others, and some will require frequent review. Keep reviewing until you can recall words to your satisfaction.

9. Reward yourself. When you have worked hard and memorized well, reward yourself. Rewards will motivate you and help you to keep striving toward your goals. Rewards should match your accomplishments. If you memorize 20 easy words, a reward is not needed; but if you memorize 20 difficult ones, a reward is in order. (More discussion of rewards appears in Chapter 10.)

A MEMORIZATION CHECKLIST

As you progress in your new language, check from time to time to see how well you are using your knowledge of memorization techniques. Circle "Yes" after the techniques you are using regularly, count one point for each technique you have tried, and rate yourself according to the scoring key below.

RATE YOUR MEMORY SKILLS

I am using the following memorization techniques in my new language:

		Score
1.	The Path to Long-term Memory and Recall	Yes _____
2.	Time Management	Yes _____
3.	Memory Goals	Yes _____
4.	SQ3R	Yes _____
5.	Association	Yes _____
6.	Mnemonics	Yes _____
7.	Chunking	Yes _____
8.	Visualization	Yes _____
9.	Planned Review	Yes _____
10.	Overlearning	Yes _____
11.	Concept Trees	Yes _____
12.	Dramatics, Body Language, and Pantomime	Yes _____
13.	Learning Modalities	Yes _____
14.	Guessing	Yes _____
15.	Rewards	Yes _____
		Total _____

Key

12–15 Good for you! You are well along the road to success in memorization.

6–11 Keep trying; keep experimenting until you find the techniques that are best for you.

0–5 Reread this chapter, and try to incorporate more of these ideas into your daily study plans.

SUMMARY

This chapter has presented the steps to long-term memory and recall through the use of memory goals and time management plans, together with a variety of memorization techniques. The first three chapters have encouraged you to think about yourself as a learner of a new language. The next three chapters focus on the language itself, beginning in Chapter 4 with the oral skills of listening and speaking; and continuing in succeeding chapters with reading and writing.

4

Using Your New Language: Listening and Speaking

Most often, people start learning a new language with the objective of communicating orally through listening and speaking. Charlie is an example of how one person developed listening and speaking skills.

Charlie expected to be transferred to Mexico in six months, and he wanted to learn Spanish so that he could communicate with the people in his office. He knew that most of them could speak English well, but it would be to his advantage if he could speak with them in Spanish. In high school he had taken two years of Spanish, but the courses had emphasized grammar and reading, and he knew very little about speaking and listening to others. He enrolled in a junior college course, which was a useful review of his high school Spanish. The instructor devoted one of every three classes to conversation, but Charlie believed he needed even more practice in speaking and listening. He borrowed tapes from the public library and listened to them in his car when he was commuting to work, but he still wanted face-to-face experiences with Spanish-speaking people.

Charlie found a little store where the employees and customers spoke Spanish. He began buying a few items and chatting with the people there. People started to include him in their conversations. Soon he could understand what people in the store were saying. He encouraged his children to study Spanish with a teacher who came to his house twice a week. Charlie and his wife began to talk to the children in Spanish, and they tried to think of ways they could speak Spanish in real-life settings. They found a local Latin American restaurant where they ordered meals in Spanish. They also began to watch the commercials and weather on cable TV in Spanish, and sometimes they understood parts of the evening news. However, they did not understand the dialogue in movies, and programs with Spanish jokes were quite beyond them. In fact, it took several years after they arrived in Mexico before they could fully enjoy these types of entertainment.

Charlie's experience shows that if you intend to develop listening and speaking skills, you may need practical experiences with your new language. Formal classes with a competent instructor give you a basis for understanding, but you can also look for outside opportunities to improve your skills. Charlie included his family in the process, and this broadened his opportunities for learning. You may be fortunate enough to enter a government or job-sponsored total immersion language program, but if not, you can develop your own immersion program by using all available resources.

LEVELS OF LISTENING

There are four levels of conversational listening ability. At the lowest level, you hear sounds but do not know when one word ends and the next begins At the second level, you can pick out words and phrases and are aware of the general topic of conversation. If you are a beginner, you will most likely reach this level after a few months, if not sooner. At the third level, you attend to the conversation, are aware of the subject, and react to many of the cues provided by speakers. At the fourth level, you become completely involved in the conversation. You remember details of the conversation, comment and argue with the speakers, and are totally engaged in the listening process. At all levels of listening, it is normal to understand much more than you can say.

You become aware of your listening ability level in unexpected ways—such as when you overhear a conversation on a bus and realize you understand what is being said. As you listen, you consciously and unconsciously absorb many words and phrases into your memory. As meanings become familiar, many of these words enter your long-term memory. Because listening plays such an important role in your vocabulary development, it should be an integral part of your study plans.

IMPROVE YOUR LISTENING

If you want to converse in your new language, careful listening is important; obviously, you have to listen and comprehend before you can respond. Even though listening is an important skill, most people do not listen carefully in everyday conversations, even in their native language. Recall the times you have misunderstood, or have been misunderstood by others, because one of you didn't listen carefully. Here are some ideas that will help you become a better listener.

The problem with listening is that after you finish listening, you usually have to respond. In order to respond, you must think of something to say; therefore, there is a tendency to stop listening in order to think of a response. This process causes difficulties in communication, because your response may be only partially related to what has been said. On the other hand, if you listen completely to what someone says and then start to respond, there may be a pause in the conversation while you think of a reply. Most people feel uncomfortable with conversational pauses. As a result, active listening to every element of a conversation is unusual. To resolve this dilemma, try to listen to as much of a conversation as possible before formulating your reply, and use the following selective listening techniques.

SELECTIVE LISTENING

Understanding a conversation is like a guessing game or an experiment. You select the words you know from the conversation and try to figure out how they go together. If you know the topic of the conversation, your selection of words will not be at random because you will select words related to the topic. This means that you do not have to pay attention to all the words you hear. If you listen to every single word, you will become confused. Just as you listen selectively in your first language, you can do the same in your new language. Practice asking yourself, "What is this conversation about?" "What is happening?" Concentrate on the main ideas and be satisfied when you understand them. As you become a better listener, you will understand more details and will be able to associate main ideas with details.

CONCENTRATION

Besides learning to listen selectively, you will improve your listening ability if you learn to concentrate on the speaker, feel well physically, and understand the speaker's body language. Listening requires concentration in order to absorb ideas. If you are distracted in any way, your listening comprehension suffers. For example, if you are in a class but cannot concentrate because of personal problems, you need to take steps to postpone thinking about your problems until after class. Select a seat where you have the best possible view of the instructor and of your classmates. Maintain eye contact; watch lip, face, and body movements; and listen more intently. Also, feeling well physically helps you to be alert and ready to listen. This means observing sensible eating, sleeping, and exercise habits that keep your body and mind in condition to concentrate.

PREPARATION

In order to understand when you listen, you need to know the vocabulary that is used. Without this knowledge, listening is a waste of time. Prepare yourself for class by memorizing key vocabulary, listening to tapes that are part of the course, and developing an appropriate vocabulary for the required activities. If you have prepared adequately and still don't understand something that is said, don't panic. Let the words flow over you like a stream of water. Relax and listen for words and phrases you know, and then try to tie them together into meanings. When you don't understand, ask the speaker to explain—interrupting on these occasions is usually perfectly all right. Ask questions every time you lose the meaning of a conversation. Don't be afraid to let your classmates know you haven't understood. Chances are that several of them didn't understand either, and they will be glad you asked for clarification.

UNDERSTANDING COMMUNICATION

Understanding body language is an important element in listening. A speaker communicates in two ways, through words and through body language. Each culture has its own body language that conveys specific meanings. For example, an English speaker looks directly into your eyes to make an important statement. If the speaker looks down or away from you, uncertainty about the truth of what is being said may be communicated. Listeners also use body language, such as nodding the head periodically to indicate that they are following the speaker, or furrowing the brow to signal that they need help understanding.

LISTENING PROBLEMS

Two special problems for beginning language learners are the speed of conversations and the variety of dialects and styles of speech. To prepare for the inevitable occasions when the conversation is too fast, learn to say "Please speak slowly" and "Please repeat." If you still do not understand, you may need to say "Please write it down." Until you have become a good listener in your new language, the speed of conversations will be a problem that you have to expect. However, experienced instructors are usually able to pace conversations to your rate of comprehension, and most speakers are accustomed to slowing down when reminded that they are talking to foreigners. Gradually, your rate of understanding will improve until you can understand native speakers at normal speed.

The different dialects and styles of speech used in your new language may be confusing for you. Usually your instructor will speak a standard variety, but people you meet may not. Upon discovering that a speaker uses an unfamiliar dialect or style, many learners automatically assume that they will not be able to understand anything the speaker says. Fortunately, this is rarely a severe problem. The differences among the varieties of a language are quite superficial, and you can soon recognize many more familiar than unfamiliar words and expressions. If you know any standard variety of your new language, you can quickly adapt to regional and stylistic varieties, and you should not be surprised or frightened when you encounter them.

SPEAKING

Although speaking with near-native proficiency is one ultimate goal of foreign language study, this goal takes years to attain, and there are several intermediate proficiency levels at which speaking ability is very satisfying and useful. Improving your speaking skills is simply a matter of practice and of realizing that progress occurs gradually and imperceptibly.

REDUCING YOUR ANXIETY

Young children experiment continuously with language and do not worry, or even seem to notice, when they make mistakes. For adults, who are accustomed to using polished language patterns, the experimentation process of early language learning may be an embarrassing, ego-deflating experience. As a language learner, you need to step fearlessly into conversations and learn to laugh at your mistakes. This is easier said than done. Some individuals actually discontinue their language studies because they are embarrassed by their mistakes. Others stop speaking in class when corrected by the instructor because they have such uncomfortable feelings about themselves and their abilities.

Successful language learning experiences are those that reduce feelings of discomfort to a minimum. You can contribute to the elimination of your own natural anxiety by trying to keep talking in your new language no matter how you feel. Learn to enjoy experimenting with your new language. If you are very fearful, tell your instructor and ask to be corrected only if your mistakes interfere with communication, which they probably won't. Then, as you gain more confidence, experiment and make mistakes. Your speaking ability will progress from one-word, stumbling utterances to smoothly spoken but memorized sentences, to conversations partly in your first language and partly in your new language, and finally to the exchange of ideas in more complex conversations.

CONQUERING PRONUNCIATION

Besides a fear of speaking in front of others, some adult learners feel uncomfortable about the pronunciation of their new language. Each language has unique sounds that you learn to hear and reproduce. Some languages have a few sounds that you cannot at first hear at all, and in any new language you can expect to encounter sounds that you are not able to reproduce exactly. Be heartened, however, by the realization that we are all born with an amazing vocal mechanism that makes it possible to imitate the sounds of new languages. While you may not be able to copy native speech exactly, you can attain acceptable pronunciation that native speakers will understand. Unless you are preparing to engage in intelligence work or other activities that require you to pass for a native speaker, you should leave the details of pronunciation to work themselves out at the higher levels of speaking proficiency.

Your instructor can identify the sounds that are troublesome for you and can tell you which of them you are not pronouncing correctly. You can then make a list of words containing these sounds at the beginning, middle, and end of words. The first step to near-native pronunciation occurs when you can pronounce these words to your instructor's satisfaction. However, don't be surprised if you can pronounce words well by themselves, but continue to have difficulty when speaking continuously. At the early stages, just saying the words is a higher priority than pronouncing them properly.

MAINTAINING A POSITIVE ATTITUDE

If you expect to live in an area where your new language is spoken, you may wonder whether native speakers will tolerate your experimentation with their language. Communication with others is not based totally on your language fluency but in large measure on your attitude toward the people and culture. If you sincerely try to communicate with others, your efforts will be noticed and you will be accepted and respected. Different cultures have different levels of tolerance of foreigners' speech and behavior, and you will need to accommodate the attitudes you find. For the most part, people in other cultures appreciate the effort required to learn a new language. In fact, friendships have been made by two people helping one another learn each other's language.

Work and play with speaking in your new language. When you were a child, learning to speak in your first language, you played games with the sounds, made up funny songs, and used language as well as you could to meet your needs. Use the same techniques in your new language. Make up word games, sing songs, talk to everyone, and reward yourself for your accomplishments. Use your growing abilities in every way possible and enjoy your new speaking skills.

SUMMARY

Listening and speaking abilities are learned gradually, and most people can understand considerably more in their new language than they can say. You will do well in oral skills if you remember that you do not have to understand every word in order to comprehend an idea, and you do not have to say everything perfectly in order to be understood.

Reading and writing are parallel in many ways to listening and speaking. The next two chapters are about reading and writing in your new language. Chapter 5 is for you only if you need to learn a new writing system, such as the ones used to write Russian or Chinese. If your new language uses a familiar alphabet, you may continue with Chapter 6.

5

Learning a New Writing System

If you have chosen to learn Russian, Chinese, Japanese, Arabic, or another language that uses an unfamiliar writing system, you have a challenging task in addition to listening, speaking, and organizing your ideas in your new language. At the beginning, you may be able to work with a special form of your new language in familiar letters, which is not normally used by speakers of the language in everyday life but which makes it easier for you to represent your new language in writing. Or you may jump into the new writing system from the beginning along with, or even before, using the language orally. In either case, before you can pick up a newspaper in your new language or any other material that is not especially written for students, or before you can write anything that could be understood by a native reader, you will need to become familiar with a new set of written characters.

UNDERSTANDING THE BACKGROUND OF DIFFERENT WRITING SYSTEMS

ALPHABETS

Most languages use *alphabets*. An alphabet is a writing system in which the symbols represent individual sounds. Since languages typically have between twenty and forty different sounds, an alphabetic system can be devised so that by using approximately one character for each sound, an unlimited number of words can be written with a manageable number of different symbols. Our alphabet was devised by the ancient Romans to write Latin, although some of its symbols can be traced back to earlier writing systems. As the Roman empire, and later the Roman church, expanded its influence, the Roman alphabet came to be used for writing the languages of peoples whose cultures were influenced by Rome. Of course, these languages had quite different sounds from Latin, so the alphabet has been adapted in different ways for different languages. For example, Latin did not have the sound that is represented in English as *sh,* so there is no historically standard way to write this sound. French writes it *ch,* German *sch,* Italian *sc,* Portuguese *x,* Polish *sz,* and Romanian *ş.*

A number of important languages use alphabets other than the Roman alphabet. In these languages the principle of writing, in which symbols correspond to sounds, is the same one we are accustomed to. Russian, for example, is written in an alphabet known as Cyrillic, which is supposed to have been developed by St. Cyril. Some of the Cyrillic characters were adapted from Greek, just as some Roman letters were. This explains why some Russian letters are identical to Roman ones in all respects, while others look like Roman letters although they correspond to different sounds. Other Cyrillic letters were especially invented for Russian. Today the Cyrillic alphabet is used to write not only Russian but also the languages of areas influenced by the Russian Orthodox Church or by Russian culture, including Bulgarian, Serbian, Ukrainian, and Mongolian.

Some other alphabetic systems you have probably heard of are Greek, Hebrew, and Arabic. Like the Roman alphabet, each has been used at one time or another to write languages other than the one for which it was devised. For example, Persian uses the Arabic alphabet even though the two languages are not historically related.

An interesting alphabet used by millions of people is Devanagari, which was devised thousands of years ago to write Sanskrit. It is used today to write Hindi and other languages of India. Unlike the alphabets just mentioned, Devanagari is not totally linear; that is, the

consonants are written below an imaginary line and the vowels that
follow the consonants are written above the line.

SYLLABARIES AND IDEOGRAPHIC SYSTEMS

A very small number of languages, including some very important languages, are written with systems that are not alphabetic. For
example, Thai and Cherokee use *syllabaries*. The characters of a syl-
labary, like those of an alphabet, represent sounds, but a different
symbol is used for each combination of consonants and vowels that
forms a syllable. It follows that syllabaries contain more symbols
than alphabets do.

The Chinese writing system is the only one in use today that is entirely *ideographic*. Chinese characters, or ideographs, stand not for
sounds but for objects and ideas. Compared with alphabets of
twenty to forty symbols, Chinese is written with thousands of different symbols, each of which is learned individually. Many of the
world's alphabets originated as ideographic systems in which pictures stood for words. It is not hard to understand why alphabets re-
placed ideographic writing almost everywhere. The Chinese writing
system has survived probably because it allows people from all parts
of China to communicate in writing, although their spoken languages are not mutually intelligible. With the ideographic characters, it is not necessary to know how a passage would sound in order
to understand its meaning.

Japanese uses a combination of Chinese ideographs and syllabic
characters. The Chinese characters are used to write content words
such as nouns, verbs, adjectives, and adverbs. One set of syllabic
characters is used together with the Chinese ideographs for writing
short words that express relationships among the words written in
the Chinese characters (prepositions and endings often carry out this
function in European languages). A second set of syllabic characters
is used for writing words of foreign origin that do not have a corre-
sponding Chinese character. A reader and writer of Japanese, then,

needs thousands of Chinese ideographs, plus two syllabaries that contain between forty and fifty symbols each.

In the remainder of this chapter, we will discuss ways in which you can apply some of the memory development techniques described in Chapter 3 to the job of learning an unfamiliar writing system. You will no doubt think up even better techniques that have personal meaning for you. These ideas are simply to get you started.

RELATING THE NEW TO THE FAMILIAR

Betty Lou Leaver, of the U.S. Department of State's Foreign Service Institute, has developed an easy way to learn the Cyrillic (Russian) alphabet in a few minutes.[1] For each letter of the Russian alphabet, Leaver has chosen a Russian word that is similar in both sound and meaning to its English equivalent. Some of these words are English words that have been borrowed into Russian, such as *engineer* and *Yankee*. Others are Russian words used in English, like *borscht* and *hooligan*. Still others originated in a third language and have been borrowed into both English and Russian, like *doctor* and *python*. Most, but not all, of these words begin with the Russian letter they have been chosen to represent.

Since none of the words is totally strange, and since there is enough similarity between the Roman and Cyrillic alphabets to provide clues, it takes only a very few minutes to be able to read the entire list in Russian. If you write each word on a filing card, you can review them in any order.

After you have become familiar with the Cyrillic letters, you will be ready to read the following list of American states in Russian. You will be surprised at your success in reading these new symbols, since you have not made any particular effort to memorize the Russian alphabet. Your success is possible because you have linked your new knowledge of the Cyrillic alphabet to familiar patterns for easy recall.

Using Familiar Words
to Learn the Cyrillic Alphabet

Russian word	English cognate	Russian Letter (s)	English Letter (s)
мама	mama	м, а	m, a
папа	papa	п	p
тарт	tart	т, р	t, r
парк	park	к	k
танк	tank	н	n
грамм	gram	г	g
газ	gas (type used by military)	з	z
космос	cosmos	о, с	o, s
космонавт	cosmonaut	в	v
доктор	doctor	д	d
питон	python	и	i (pr. ee)
жамр	giraffe	ж	zh
жираф	giraffe	ф	f
инженер	engineer	е	e
азимут	azimuth	у	u (pr. oo)
кэнгеру	kangaroo	э	eh
телефон	telephone	л	l
янки	Yankee	я	ya
Вашингтон	Washington	ш	sh
принц	prince	ц	ts
бензин	benzine (gas for cars)	б	b
хулиган	hooligan	х	kh
лейтенант	lieutenant	я	(no sound, dipthongizes preceding vowel)
борщ	borscht	щ	shch
рын-тын-тын	Rin-tin-tin	ы	y
дебютант	debutante	ю	yu
Чехословашкия	Czechoslovakia	ч	ch
объект	object	ъ	(indicates preceding consonant is hard)
фильм	film	ь	(indicates preceding consonant is soft, i.e. tongue raised toward palate)

Used by permission of the American Council on the Teaching of Foreign Languages.

Reading the Cyrillic Alphabet with Ease

Монтана (Montana)	Висконсин (Wisconsin)
Аляска (Alaska)	Иллиной (Illinois)
Вермонт (Vermont)	Индиана (Indiana)
Алабама (Alabama)	Орегон (Oregon)
Нью-Йорк (New York)	Юта (Utah)
Калифорния (California)	Оклахома (Oklahoma)
Айдахо (Idaho)	Саут Дакота (S. Dakota)
Саут Каролайна (S. Carolina)	Виржиния (Virginia)
Норт Дакота (N. Dakota)	Охайо (Ohio)
Вайоминг (Wyoming)	Нью Мексико (New Mexico)
Вашингтон (Washington)	Теннесси (Tennessee)
Мейн (Maine)	Арканса (Arkansas)
Коннектикут (Connecticut)	Мизуры (Missouri)
Род Айланд (Rhode Island)	Миссиссиппи (Mississippi)
Флорида (Florida)	Колорадо (Colorado)
Жоржа (Georgia)	Невада (Nevada)
Техас (Texas)	Мэриленд (Maryland)
Аризона (Arizona)	Миннесота (Minnesota)
Айова (Iowa)	Нью Джерси (New Jersey)
Массачусетс (Massachusetts)	Кентукки (Kentucky)
Пеннсильвания (Pennsylvania)	Луизиана (Louisiana)
Нью Хэмпшир (New Hampshire)	Делавэр (Delaware)
Норт Каролайна (N. Carolina)	Хаваи (Hawaii)
Небраска (Nebraska)	Мичиган (Michigan)
Канзас (Kansas)	

USING IMAGERY

Imagery is another way to help you unlock the mysteries of a new writing system. A California teacher, Zev Bar-lev, has developed a system for learning the Hebrew alphabet by using imagery and pictures.[2] Bar-lev begins with short words whose meaning is the basis for a drawing. The parts of the drawing correspond to the letters, and they help you remember and learn the new set of symbols. For example, to represent the Hebrew word for "king," Bar-lev has drawn the following hieroglyphic:

Examples here and below used by permission of *Visible Language*.

The standard printed form of the word for "king" is as follows:

מלך

Since Hebrew is written from right to left, and the word for "king" is pronounced *melekh,* the imagery of the hieroglyphic serves as an aid to memorization.

Relating Images to Learn Hebrew Symbols

מ = **m**, and is represented as a person prostrated before a king

ל = **l**, and is represented by a seated king

ך = **kh**, and is represented by a throne

The Hebrew alphabet, like all alphabets, is based on sound, but in this method you learn the meaning of the word first and you can read the Hebrew word before you know how it is pronounced. You see the word as a whole, and only afterward learn the sound and associate individual letters with their sounds. Once you have learned a few Hebrew letters, Bar-lev presents you with some familiar biblical names written in Hebrew. With little effort you can match these with their English equivalents. You have used imagery to remember the sound-symbol correspondences with no special struggle, and then by associating the new symbols with familiar sounds, you can read in your new alphabet!

For any new alphabet, you can think up your own picture drawings. The trick is to relate them to the *meanings* of some key words that produce images to help you recall the new symbols.

SOME HELP WITH CHINESE CHARACTERS

The task of learning Chinese ideographic characters is formidable because there are so many. Sometimes the history of the characters can suggest a memory aid because the early forms of the characters were more realistic pictures than the stylized ideographs used today. For example, the character for "rake" is

The character is composed of two parts. The first part is the symbol for "tree," whose historical form was

The second part is the character for "snake" or "boa," whose historical form symbolizes a boa raised on its tail:

This character evolved because the word for "rake" in Chinese sounds like the word for "boa." The snake part of the rake ideograph has nothing to do with the meaning of the word, but is there to remind readers of the pronunciation.[3]

Once you know a few Chinese characters, you begin to recognize patterns and look for them. The memorization task is less formidable because you begin to link new shapes to known ones.

SUMMARY

The secret of learning a new writing system is to start with what is familiar to you; this usually involves meanings, and therefore whole words, rather than the forms of individual symbols. From this starting point, your imagination can help you build on your knowledge of the new writing system. As you develop your imagery and memorization techniques, you discover that you can read and write in your new language with much less effort than you expected.

Be prepared to discover that handwritten characters in your new writing system may look quite different from the printed forms. You can use the same techniques to become familiar with handwritten language that you use to learn printed forms. If you already know the printed forms, you can look for similarities between print and handwriting as a basis for associating the two.

Now you can get down to the real business of reading and writing in your new language: finding out what people have to say on paper and communicating your own ideas in written form. The next chapter offers suggestions to help you get involved in those activities.

6

Using Your New Language: Reading and Writing

When you begin to study a new language, the primary focus is usually on listening and speaking because these are the skills you need initially to survive in a foreign setting. As you begin to understand conversations and are able to talk to people, you naturally want to read and write in your new language. At first, you read short items like signs, public notices, and newspaper headlines or advertisements. As your reading ability improves, you read a greater variety of longer texts, including personal notes and letters, newspaper and magazine reports, and stories or novels. For many people, a big difference between the experiences of learning their first and second languages is that in the second language, reading ability soon surpasses the skills of understanding and speaking.

This chapter will give you a variety of ideas for using your skills not only in reading, but in writing as well. The first part of the chapter discusses reading comprehension and ways to expand your reading beyond textbooks and materials especially prepared for students. The second part of the chapter discusses techniques that will enable you, as a beginning language learner, to write short letters and compositions with confidence.

READING IN YOUR NEW LANGUAGE

If you are fortunate enough to be learning your new language in a total immersion environment, you will be surrounded by things to read, in both formal and informal situations. If you are learning on your own or in a classroom, your reading resources will be your textbook, and perhaps simple newspaper and magazine articles. Whatever your situation, you need to understand what you read. Three techniques that can help you comprehend written texts are comprehending major and minor ideas, annotating, and guessing the meanings of words and ideas.

COMPREHENDING MAJOR AND MINOR IDEAS

The four steps involved in comprehending major and minor ideas help you analyze ideas carefully. In a second language, they help you focus your attention away from individual words and toward ideas.

Step One

Preview a reading selection to find the most important words. Usually, the most important words are those used in the title, table of contents, and chapter headings; subheadings, captions, italics, or other differing typefaces. Note or circle these key words and be sure you know what they mean. After you have identified these words, write down what you believe to be the major ideas presented by these important words.

Step Two

Now read the title of the selection and turn it into a question. If the title is ''Prelude to Disaster,'' your question might be ''What happened before the disaster?'' Next, skim as quickly as possible through the selection and try to find the answer to your question. If the answer is in the text, underline it with colored pencil. If the answer is not found specifically in the text, write in the margin what you believe it to be after you have skimmed the text. Finally, reread the selection more carefully and determine whether your question was really the key idea of the text. If not, what was the key idea?

Step Three

The minor ideas are those that strengthen your knowledge of the main ideas. Begin your search for minor ideas by reading the selection again. As you reread, draw a concept tree or pictorial representation of the ideas you find. (Concept trees were discussed in

Chapter 3.) Draw the major ideas first and add minor ideas as they occur in your reading. If the selection does not lend itself to the development of a concept tree, write the major and minor ideas in a standard or an organizational model outline form.

Standard Outline Form

    I. Major Idea
        A. Minor Idea
            1. Subidea
            2. Subidea
        B. Minor Idea
   II. Major Idea
        A. Minor Idea
            1. Subidea
            2. Subidea
        B. Minor Idea

Organizational Model Outline Form

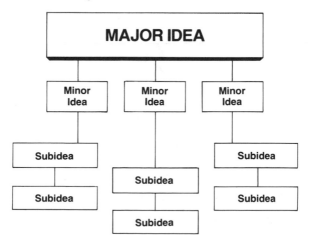

In the following concept tree, the first major idea placed on the tree was "Man notices cracks in bridge." The minor ideas related to this event were added next: "Man radios Coast Guard" and "Man rushes to bridge entrance." The subidea was then written: "No one listens." Notice how the concept tree begins with important words and grows with each idea. By looking at the tree, you can easily see the progression of important events in the story. Experiment with drawing trees until you find methods that clarify for you the major and minor ideas.

Concept Tree of Major and Minor Ideas

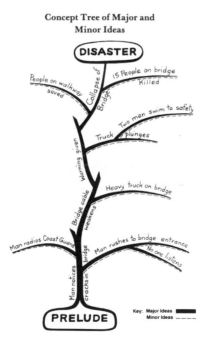

Step Four

In order to retain the understanding of major and minor ideas, you need to review. One way to review is by visualizing your concept tree and then drawing it from memory. You can also write a summary of the selection in your new language or in your native language or just write the key words and think about the minor ideas in relation to the major ideas.

As you go through the four steps, do not take time to look up unfamiliar words unless you are unable to find the major and minor ideas. Your objective in reading any selection is to understand ideas, not words.

ANNOTATING

When you annotate a textbook or other selection, you mark it in a way that clearly sets off the major and minor ideas. The following steps can help you quickly comprehend a text.

1. Circle main ideas.

2. Underline supporting details or minor ideas.

3. Underline and number a series of major or minor ideas.

4. Write a question mark in the margin if you find an idea you do not understand.

5. Bracket words or phrases you want to memorize.

6. Draw a star in the margin beside ideas you want to remember.

7. Write comments in the margins.

8. Summarize the total passage or selection at the top or bottom of the page.

The following is an example of an annotation in a Spanish textbook. Notice how the major idea in this selection on driving in Mexico stands out and the minor ideas are easy to find.

Para poder conducir en México Ud. necesita tener la licencia internacional de conducir, aunque aquellas personas que tienen licencia de los Estados Unidos, pueden utilizarla también en México.

El seguro de automóvil de su país no es válido para México, y es necesario obtener un seguro especial. Esto lo puede hacer en la misma frontera mexicana, o bien a través de su propio agente de seguros.

Si Ud. tiene problemas con su vehículo en territorio mexicano, puede recurrir a la patrulla *Angeles Verdes*, cuya función es ayudar a los conductores de manera gratuito en caso de averías del coche, accidentes u otras emergencias relacionadas con su vehículo.

From Juan Kattán-Ibarra, *Basic Spanish Conversation: A Functional Approach* (Lincolnwood, IL: National Textbook Company, 1985), p.67.

GUESSING FOR MEANING

Sensible, logical guessing will save you time and effort when you are reading in your new language. You can expect to encounter words whose meanings you do not know. When you come to an unfamiliar word, do not immediately look it up. Instead, guess its probable meaning in relation to the main ideas of the context, to the social and cultural setting of the selection, and to what you already know about the subject. If you stop to look up the meaning of unfamiliar words, you interrupt the flow of ideas and you may lose the total meaning of an idea. Make rational, intelligent guesses as you do when reading in your native language.

For example, read the following: ''Mary was *loquacious* in conversing with Joan and Annette. She told them all about her adventures.'' You could guess from the context that *loquacious* has to do with the way Mary talked and is likely to mean ''fast,'' ''a lot,'' or ''careful.'' All of these guesses are reasonable, but only one is right. As you read on, the correct meaning may be clarified from the context, and you would not need to use a dictionary. Usually, you will need to understand about 80 percent of the major ideas in order to make sense of a reading selection. The remaining ideas may be guessed from context.

Your guesses may be incorrect and may lead to incorrect assumptions about meaning; however, guessing is a legitimate part of the reading process and should be used whenever possible.

READING BEYOND THE TEXTBOOK

If you study only your assigned textbook, you will obtain a limited and artificial reading knowledge of your new language. If your reading ability in your new language is to grow, you should read material you have chosen for yourself. Wide reading, especially about topics that interest you, is the best way to increase your vocabulary and your comprehension of written texts.

You may wonder what a beginning learner can find to read. If you read newspapers in your native language, you are familiar with newspaper style. You can use your knowledge to guess the meanings of words and ideas in newspapers in your new language. Advertisements are similar all over the world; for this reason they are usually a good place to start reading in a new language. Weather reports contain graphs, pictures, and diagrams with obvious clues to many terms such as *temperature, rain, wind,* and *humidity.* Television program listings are often easy to follow and contain references to familiar movies and dramatic series.

As your reading ability improves, look for other reading resources. Public and college libraries often receive magazines, newspapers, and books in a variety of languages, as do many bookstores.

Travel bureaus, government agencies, and industries may be a good source of pamphlets in your new language. You will find that something you enjoy and find interesting will be remembered and understood more easily than a text that is assigned in a class. Nevertheless, your required reading and assignments should receive top priority in your time management plans.

Through your expanded reading program, your abilities in all aspects of your new language will grow, and you will soon become an excellent reader.

WRITING

Like reading, writing in a new language is a global process that involves communicating ideas rather than words. This thought underlies the following discussion of the writing process in terms of getting started, developing your writing, and polishing your writing. After this discussion, three aspects of your new language will be mentioned, all of which are specifically related to writing: the use of dictionaries, spelling, and the role of grammar in writing.

STARTING TO WRITE

When you sit down to write a letter or composition in your new language, begin by writing one or two key ideas; then, give yourself a five- or ten-minute time limit and write as many ideas about your topic as you can. Since writing is not a straightforward process, you may begin anywhere—the middle, the end, or even the beginning of your composition. Later, you will fill in the missing parts.

Use a pencil with an eraser, an erasable pen, or a word processor; and be prepared to change, delete, and add to what you have written. Your level of ability in your new language should not inhibit the writing process. Write as much as you can in your new language and write the rest in your native language. When your composition is more nearly completed, you can use reference sources as you revise it.

As you write, pretend you are an artist creating a picture. Write dabs of ideas on your paper, the way an artist applies dabs of paint on a canvas. Some dabs will appear at the top, and others at the end. Leave spaces for adding more ideas, and fill your page with sentences, phrases, and words related to the ideas you want to express.

What should you do if you cannot think of enough ideas to make up a short letter or even a paragraph? The act of writing itself will help you formulate ideas starting from your initial idea. Writing seems to beget writing. The secret is to keep writing, and keep your hand moving, and while you write, to formulate what you are going to write next.

Some people need to think through their total composition first, and write an outline of what they hope to say. If you need to do this, give yourself a time limit of five or ten minutes to write your outline. However, a preplanned outline and a good introduction to your topic are not needed in order to start writing. These elements may even inhibit your ability to create new ideas, and they may limit the scope of your writing. All you really need is one idea and a determination to keep writing. Some people find that the use of a typewriter or a word processor keeps ideas flowing. Experiment until you find a procedure that helps you write many ideas quickly and efficiently. Consider the experience of Tom and Jim, when faced with a writing assignment.

> Tom needed to write a paragraph for a class assignment. He wanted to begin with an excellent opening sentence, but he could not think of one. He had no idea how to begin, and became discouraged. His classmate, Jim, couldn't think of a good first sentence, either, but he had an idea for an ending, so he jotted it down. Then Jim discovered that he could write his paragraph from the end to the middle, and at last, when the paragraph had taken shape, he added a first sentence.

When you have difficulty generating ideas, write anything that comes to mind. From these ideas, more ideas will come forth, and you will develop a good composition.

After completing the first stage of your composition, you will have ideas written in sentences, phrases, and words scattered on your page. The next step is to develop your writing into a cohesive whole with major and minor ideas stated clearly.

DEVELOPING YOUR WRITING

Read what you have already written, and decide which ideas belong at the beginning, middle, and end. Give yourself five or ten minutes to place your ideas in a logical order; then reread and continue rewriting until the ideas seem logical and you are satisfied with the organization.

POLISHING YOUR WRITING

Most likely you have been writing in your native language as well as in your new language, and your final step will be to express everything in your new language. Because you are a learner, your writing will inevitably contain traces of your native language, as well as other features that make it obvious that you are not a native writer of your new language. Don't worry about writing like a native. What you should do in revising your writing is to be conscious of your audience. Will your writing be read by your instructor or by a family member? Use the language patterns the reader would expect you to use.

Although your attention should be on the organization and expression of your ideas, rather than on the forms of your new language, this is the time to make sure that verbs agree with subjects, that irregular verbs have been properly used, and that little words—like the equivalents of *the, a,* and *for*—are in their proper place.

If you are in a class, ask your instructor and other class members to read your composition and make suggestions about your writing. Ask them to tell you if the main ideas are clear, if minor ideas support major ideas logically, and if the ideas are stated in language appropriate for the intended audience.

IMPROVING YOUR WRITING ABILITY

Your writing ability will improve if you write regularly and read the types of materials you want to write. If you wish to become proficient in writing letters, read letters in your new language. If you want to write scientific papers, read scientific papers. Reading familiarizes you with the language structures, conventions, and vocabulary of the type of writing you want to do. Gradually these elements become part of your knowledge, and you begin to write in similar ways. This is a long-term process, but if you work at it regularly, you will begin to notice improvement in your writing ability.

EXPANDING YOUR WRITING SKILLS

Three aspects of learning and using a new language that are particularly related to the development of writing ability are dictionaries, spelling, and grammar. The last sections of this chapter will discuss these in relation to the writing process.

The Use of Dictionaries

Four kinds of dictionaries are useful sources of words and meanings: monolingual dictionaries, bilingual dictionaries, dictionaries of synonyms, and pictorial dictionaries.

A monolingual dictionary is written entirely in your new language. It gives you definitions of words and is useful for looking up the meanings of words you do not know, provided you can read well enough in your new language to understand the definitions. A bilingual dictionary, such as English-French, translates words but assumes you already know the definitions in one language or the other.

Bilingual dictionaries usually give several possible translations for each item, and the user has to choose the appropriate one; therefore, you have to be careful because you may not have a way to be sure you have chosen the correct equivalent. Suppose you were writing a business report in Spanish and wanted to know the word for *brand* in order to write that consumers have favorite brands of products. Upon looking up *brand* in an English-Spanish/Spanish-English bilingual dictionary, you would find no fewer than nine equivalents. Two of the equivalents are labeled "poetic," so you could eliminate them without knowing anything else about them. You could eliminate some of the other inappropriate translations by checking them in the Spanish-English half of the dictionary, where you might learn that some refer to branding cattle, and others to insults. The appropriate word, *marca,* is glossed as "manufacturer's mark," among other equivalents. You would eventually be able to settle on it as the best translation for *brand* in the context you intended. Once you have found a word in a bilingual dictionary, checking its meaning in a monolingual dictionary in your new language is a useful way to be sure you have found the word you really wanted.

Dictionaries of synonyms are available for most languages and can help you find a variety of words to use in writing. You do have to start with at least one word in your new language that is related to the concept about which you are seeking new words. Dictionaries of synonyms can be used as you would use *Roget's Thesaurus* in English, since there is no exact equivalent of that tool in other languages.

Pictorial dictionaries are available for most European languages. The most famous is the *Duden,* which was developed by a nineteenth-century German lexicographer of the same name. It divides the world of experience into categories and provides a complex drawing for each category. It is useful when you need a term that is hard to find in a bilingual dictionary, such as *bath mat.* A bilingual dictionary would have a listing for *bath* and one for *mat,* but would not necessarily tell you how to put them together. In a pictorial dictionary you can turn to the page depicting a bathroom, find the bath mat in the drawing, and read its name in your new language.

Intelligent use of dictionaries can help you avoid difficulties in writing, as in the following example:

> Gerald was writing in Spanish about the bombing of Pearl
> Harbor. Not wanting to overuse the word *barco* for "boat," he looked
> up *vessel* in the English section of his bilingual dictionary. The very
> first equivalent listed was *vasija,* which is actually a vessel used for
> carrying water. Gerald assumed that the first equivalent would most
> likely be the best, so he wrote the following: "Many water jugs were
> destroyed in the bombing of Pearl Harbor." The word that Gerald
> would have wanted, *buque,* actually was listed next-to-last among the
> various equivalents of *vessel.* Gerald could have avoided this error if
> he had referred to the Spanish section of his bilingual dictionary or to
> an all-Spanish dictionary and checked *vasija.* He also could have
> consulted the naval section of a pictorial dictionary.

Knowing how to use dictionaries is a valuable skill in writing in a second language. You should be familiar with all four types of dictionaries.

Spelling

Fortunately, most languages are considerably easier to spell than English. The words of most languages, with the notable exception of French, can be spelled correctly if you know how to pronounce them, and pronounced correctly if you can see the spelling. Since good spelling is so closely related to good pronunciation and because your first contact with many new words will be through reading the words rather than hearing them, it is to your advantage to make an effort to spell accurately in your new language. Spelling is important to your writing also because spelling inaccuracies tend to distract readers' attention from the writer's ideas.

Spelling in a new language, as in your first language, is most easily acquired by using your best learning modality—visual, oral, tactile, or a combination of all three. However, the more closely the spelling of your language is related to the pronunciation, the more effective an oral approach to spelling will be. Here are some ideas that may be effective for your particular needs.

1. Visual approach
   a. Look at a word for 30 seconds.
   b. Close your eyes and visualize the word on a piece of paper or a chalkboard, written in large letters.
   c. Compare your visual image with a written one.
   d. If your visual image is not clear, look at the word again until you can visualize it clearly.

2. Oral approach
   a. Look at a word.
   b. Say the word aloud.
   c. Sound out the parts or syllables of the word.
   d. Spell the word aloud.
   e. Compare your oral spelling with the written word.

3. Tactile approach
   a. Look at a word.
   b. Copy it twice.
   c. Write the word once from memory.
   d. Compare your spelling with the source.
   e. Write the word four more times from memory.
   f. Check for accuracy.
4. Combination approach
   a. Visualize a word, noting especially the first and last letters.
   b. Write the word.
   c. Say the word aloud.
   d. Close your eyes and visualize the word.
   e. Check to be certain your visual image is accurate.
   f. Write the word in a sentence.

One of these methods, or a combination of them, used regularly will help you develop strong spelling skills.

Grammar

Grammar has deliberately been left to the end of this chapter on reading and writing, because if you are just beginning to learn a new language, comprehension and expression of ideas should come first. The real test of your knowledge of the new language is your ability to understand and communicate with native speakers. Grammar plays a smaller part in this ability than listening, speaking, reading, and vocabulary. However, the editorial skills obtained from conscious knowledge of the grammar of your new language can undeniably make your writing more authentic. Grammar rules come in at the last stage of writing, that of polishing your writing.

All languages have patterns, rules, and systems that are learned more easily if you understand how the rules are interconnected. When studying the forms and rules of grammar, you should make your own meaningful tables based on your listening, speaking, and reading knowledge. For example, if your language has different verb forms for person and number of the verb's subject, you would probably want to highlight the forms for *I* and *you* subjects, since at first you will need them more than the other possibilities. If you can relate rules to what you already know, the rules will make sense and will be remembered. If you just try to memorize rules abstractly, you will probably forget them quickly.

Ideally, a grammar rule should be learned when you need to say or write something that requires the rule, rather than when you have reached the page in a textbook that explains it. Use grammar to enhance your understanding of speaking and writing patterns in your new language, not simply as a set of exercises. Grammar exercises are often easy to complete, but you should not assume that because you can do exercises, you will automatically write well. As you have seen, writing is a much more global process than the completion of exercises.

SUMMARY

The first three chapters of this book focused on the most important factor in acquiring your new language — you. Chapters 4 and 6 have been concerned with various aspects of the language itself as it relates to you, the learner. Reading and writing have been viewed in the discussion just concluded as the search for the understanding and expression of ideas, and suggestions for development of your reading and writing skills have been offered with this goal in mind.

In the next group of chapters, several factors will be considered that are external both to you and to your new language, but which can play a large part in language acquisition and learning. The most important of these factors is your instructor. Chapter 7 will suggest how you can get the best help and support from the person who will be probably the main source from which your language acquisition will develop. Continuing with teacher-related suggestions, Chapter 8 is about test-taking skills in foreign languages. Then, Chapter 9 introduces some technological aids that have the potential to support the development of skills in your new language.

7

You and
Your Instructor

Many people begin learning a new language by studying on their own. However, unless you live where you can use your new language daily, you will probably work with an instructor, either in a formal class or privately. Your instructor can analyze your present knowledge and your style of learning and can help you plan your studies. An instructor can also monitor your progress, encourage you when the work is difficult, and answer your questions. Your instructor serves as a model for the way the language is used and also introduces you to the culture of the countries where your new language is spoken. Because your instructor is of such importance to your learning, you should choose an instructor carefully. The next section will give you some ideas for doing this.

CHOOSING AN INSTRUCTOR

Before making a commitment to study with a particular instructor, you would want ideally to interview the instructor, as well as former students, to discover the instructor's goals and teaching style. If possible, the instructor's goals and teaching style should match your needs and objectives. If you want to be able to speak well, look for an instructor who emphasizes oral proficiency; if you want to read scientific papers, find instruction that emphasizes translation and scientific vocabulary. If you learn best through visual, oral, or tactile methods, look for an instructor who uses these techniques.

Research in recent years has shown that people learn a foreign language best when instruction includes oral communication in real-life settings in the new language, with emphasis on listening to authentic speech to develop a feel for the natural sounds and rhythms of the language. You are likely to progress faster if beginning instruction does not overemphasize grammar. Grammar is learned gradually after many experiences communicating with your instructor, other students, and native speakers. A classroom where you are free to make errors without correction and where anxiety levels are low, coupled with many opportunities to experiment with your new language by listening, speaking, reading, and writing, seems to enhance the quality and rate of learning. Therefore, look for an instructor who uses classroom and recorded drills only to reinforce communicative skills and who will evaluate you on your communicative abilities rather than on your ability to perform repetitive exercises.

KNOWING YOUR INSTRUCTOR

Your instructor is the person who can help you most in your studies, so you need to learn to communicate with your instructor regularly and frequently. Since an instructor is unlikely to approach you unless there has been a crisis such as failing an important exam, you should take the initiative to keep your instructor informed of your needs and progress. It is especially important not to wait until you have built up a record of failure or discouragement; talk to your instructor and seek help.

Gwen, who was studying German, missed several classes because she was ill. When she returned to class, she felt lost and became discouraged. She decided to take the initiative and made an appointment to see her instructor. Because she had missed some important classes, the instructor referred her to a graduate student for coaching. Her instructor also encouraged her to interrupt and ask questions in class so he would know when she hadn't understood. After a few weeks of coaching, Gwen was able to keep up with the class, and was glad she had talked to her instructor and sought his advice.

When you need help, make an appointment with your instructor; be businesslike and ask specific questions about the things you need to know. Abide by office hours, and do not wear out your welcome by consuming too much office time or talking about personal problems. If you have personal problems, make an appointment with a counselor, nurse, or physician who is more qualified in this area than your language instructor.

RECOGNIZING WHEN TO SEEK HELP

Several warning signals may indicate the need for help in learning your new language. Among these are feelings of anxiety, embarrassment, frustration, boredom, and fatigue. You may also be doing poorly on exams and quizzes. If you experience any of these warning signals, it is time to talk to your instructor. Do not wait until it is too late to seek help. Here is a questionnaire that should help you decide whether you need help.

RATE YOUR NEED FOR HELP

1. I already know the content of the course and find the classes boring.   Yes   No

2. I do not have the background knowledge necessary for success in this course.   Yes   No

3. I find this course unrelated to things that are meaningful to me.   Yes   No

4. I have difficulty learning because of the instructor's style and methods.   Yes   No

5. I have failed or made low grades on a quiz or mid-term exam.   Yes   No

6. I have missed so many classes, I do not know what to do.   Yes   No

7. I rarely finish my assignments.   Yes   No

8. I can't keep up with the required memorization.   Yes   No

9. I don't understand what the instructor or students are saying.   Yes   No

10. I am embarrassed when I speak in class.   Yes   No

11. I feel anxious in this class.   Yes   No

12. I have so many personal problems that my studies
   are suffering.   Yes   No

13. I am so fatigued, or feel so ill, that I can't do my
   work.   Yes   No

Key

If you checked "Yes" for any item between 1 and 11, make an appointment to talk to your instructor. The statements you checked can be given to your instructor as the reason for the appointment. If you checked "Yes" for item 12, make an appointment with a counselor; and if you checked "Yes" for item 13, visit your school nurse or a physician.

Before you talk to your instructor, think of specific things you would like the instructor to do to help you. Suppose you already know the content of the course and you find the class boring; ask to be moved to a more advanced class, or if this is impossible, ask your instructor to give you individualized assignments so that you may progress at your own rate. If you do not have the necessary background for the class, ask to change to a lower level class, or ask for special coaching. Also ask the instructor if there are any books, programmed study materials, or technological aids that might help you catch up with the class.

If the course work is unrelated to subjects that are meaningful to you, ask the instructor to include relevant materials in your assignments. Alternatively, you may inquire about switching to another class that is more compatible with your goals. If you believe that the instructor's style and methods are the source of your problem, you may need to enroll in a different class.

If you have been missing and have rarely been able to finish assignments, you should reassess your time management plans, read the section on procrastination in Chapter 11 of this book, and then talk to your instructor, who may have other suggestions.

If you don't understand what the instructor or other students say in class, don't be afraid to ask them to speak slower, repeat, or clarify. Perhaps you have not kept up with learning vocabulary, or perhaps the pace of the class is too fast for you. Get advice from your

instructor about extra listening practice, possibly with tape recordings, or about the possibility of changing to another class.

If you are anxious or embarrassed, it is possible that the class is
conducted in a manner that causes these reactions. It may also be
that you are the only class member who is affected. If the class is conducted in a way that causes you distress, it may be prudent to look
for another instructor. If changing instructors is not possible or appropriate, ask your instructor to help you by avoiding the events
that produce feelings of anxiety. For example, you can ask to be
called on only when you volunteer, and then promise yourself that
you will volunteer more often. If your anxiety persists, you may
benefit from a stress management seminar designed to help people
cope with stress-related anxieties.

IF YOUR INSTRUCTOR CANNOT HELP YOU

Possibly, you may have an instructor who cannot help you. Your
goals or learning styles may not match the instructor's, or you may
have a personal or academic problem that is beyond the instructor's
ability to solve. More often than we would wish, language instructors are not trained to analyze your learning styles or to approach
problems in more than one way. Some instructors set unrealistic
goals and present language as a puzzle to be solved rather than as a
vehicle for communication. Even though many learners adapt to
this situation and enjoy solving puzzles and analyzing complex systems of thought, you may have to consider yourself unlucky in the
choice of instructor and think about dropping the course. Before you
do, however, assess your real reasons for difficulties. Do not use the
instructor as a scapegoat for lack of enthusiasm or inadequate time
management.

If your instructor cannot help you, there are people who can. In
most colleges and schools there are counselors who specialize in academic problems, and other counselors who specialize in personal
problems. Turn to these professionals, and find out what services
they offer. Personal counselors help you over extended periods with
a variety of problems. Academic counselors can help you choose
classes and avoid unsuitable courses. Even though they probably do
not speak your new language, academic counselors can help you

find a tutor or coach for individual assistance. Most college counseling centers offer seminars and workshops in study skills, stress management, career choices, and the reentry problems of older students. If your instructor cannot help you, turn to these excellent support services.

SUMMARY

If you analyze your personal learning situation and take the initiative in bringing your concerns to the instructor's attention, your instructor may be your best personal resource in learning your new language. If your instructor cannot help you, other sources of professional assistance may not be far away.

One occasion when you really need to know your instructor is at the time of an exam or test. The next chapter offers suggestions for taking tests in stride and turning them into additional learning opportunities.

8

Taking Tests Successfully

If taking tests is part of your foreign language class, or if you intend to take a standardized proficiency test, this chapter will help you prepare for and take tests successfully. Most of the discussion refers to ordinary classroom tests and quizzes devised by the instructor for a particular class. The chapter concludes with some observations about standardized placement and proficiency exams prepared or administered by someone other than your classroom instructor.

PREPARING FOR TESTS

Preparing for a test is like getting ready for a party; the more information you have, the better you can prepare. No one wants to be the poor soul in the gorilla suit when the other guests are in tuxedos and gowns. Before you can prepare for a quiz or test, you need to know the following information.

1. What is the content of the test? What specific items should be reviewed or memorized? Which sections of books or tapes and which vocabulary items are the basis for the test? Will specific subject matter be covered in addition to communication skills?

2. What is the format of the test? Is it oral or written? If the test is oral, exactly how will it be conducted? Will oral questions be tape-recorded or asked "live" by the examiner? Will you be expected to carry on a conversation or write from dictation? If the test is written, will answers be true/false, multiple choice, single-word responses, sentences, or essays? Will you be asked to translate?

3. How will the test be graded? What weight will be given to different sections of the test? What score will be required to pass?

4. When will the test take place? How long will it take?

5. Can you examine previous tests in order to note style and content?

Additionally, you can make educated guesses about the content and style of a test in several ways, directly and indirectly.

1. Read the course objectives and estimate which of them are likely to be tested. Ask your instructor to discuss the objectives of the course and of the test. Phrasing your request for information in terms of objectives is more reasonable and acceptable than asking what questions will appear on a test. If your instructor has not discussed objectives for a particular test, a pleasant inquiry about when this discussion might occur is perfectly correct.

2. Analyze recent assignments and expect the test to be related closely to those activities.

3. Review recent class activities. What have you been practicing in class? If you have been practicing describing the use of kitchen implements, expect to do it on the test, perhaps in a different way. For example, if you have discussed in class the utensils you would need to bake a pie, it would be reasonable on a test to describe what you would need to make a cake.

4. Analyze your instructor's style of communication so that on oral tests you will be more at ease. How many times is your instructor willing to repeat a question? How are questions phrased? Are you expected to answer in complete sentences, or is a one-word answer sufficient?

FOLLOWING DAILY STUDY PLANS

After you know what the test will be about, plan your study strategies accordingly. If you have been following the study ideas in this book, you will not need to do many things differently before a test from what you have been doing all along. However, you may wish to focus especially on the parts of the course that will be tested. You can space reviews so that you go over the appropriate material before the day of the test and possibly increase the amount of time devoted to practicing your new language within your time management plans.

If you will be tested orally, practice speaking in front of a mirror or practice with a partner, and record your voice so that you can experience oral testing conditions before you take the test. Participate actively in class, because class activities are likely to prepare you for the test. Be certain you have learned the appropriate vocabulary so that you can converse easily.

COPING WITH TEST ANXIETY

Everyone experiences some anxiety when taking a test. A little anxiety is beneficial because it stimulates your awareness and thought processes. However, some people, even when they are well prepared, experience anxiety that is detrimental to success. When these individuals study for an exam, they begin to think that they can never learn the material; and when they first look at a test, they may believe there is nothing on the test that they know how to answer. Panic ensues. If this has happened to you, it is important to take time before a test to explore your thoughts and feelings about testing. You can change your attitudes by following anxiety reduction methods that have worked for many people.

Jeff has learned to use his physical signs of anxiety as cues for action. When Jeff notices tension rising in his body before or during a test, he takes a few deep breaths, identifies the particular muscle groups in his body that are tense, and then deliberately relaxes and tenses them a few times. He concentrates his thoughts on the smooth, warm feeling of his relaxed muscles. He has found that concentrating on the muscles from the base of the neck across his shoulders reduces tension. He tenses and relaxes his muscles until he feels better. He has also found that tension and anxiety tend to dissipate when he says the word *calm* to himself several times.

As Jeff begins to relax and feel less anxious, he tries to explore the ideas and thought patterns that coincide with his anxiety. Usually these thoughts are negative, self-defeating, and illogical. For example, as Jeff reads the first few items on the test, he may become tense because he does not immediately know all of the answers. He assumes that the rest of the test will be as difficult. He has even thought to himself that his friends will consider him stupid for not having studied well enough to pass the test! Within a short period of time he has allowed his negative thoughts to control his actions, and he can no longer think rationally.

Because Jeff has been determined to change his thinking patterns and his attitudes toward tests, he has taught himself to listen for negative self-talk, to laugh at these ideas, and to challenge the part of himself that forecasts the future negatively. He has learned to control anxiety by challenging his logic and asking himself such questions as "What evidence do I have that will support this negative idea?" After he has challenged his thoughts, he has found that focusing on the test helps him to relax and complete the test successfully.

To summarize, Jeff takes the following steps to break the chain reaction of negative thoughts:

1. He laughs at his negative ideas.
2. He challenges his logic by stating, "This is not true. I can do it. I can succeed."
3. He tenses and relaxes his muscles, and he concentrates his thoughts on the warm feeling of the relaxed muscles.
4. He focuses his attention on the subject matter in order to avoid thinking negatively.

Try these techniques when you begin to feel anxious. Relax and concentrate on the positive aspects of your ability, and success will follow.

USING YOUR TIME WISELY BEFORE THE TEST

Here are some ideas that may help you during the twenty-four hours before a test.

Complete a final review of difficult vocabulary and other important material likely to be tested. Get a good night's sleep. Relax with the knowledge that your systematic studying and your sequenced, daily memorization will reward you with dividends on your test. Look forward to the test as a challenge for which you have all the tools necessary for success. Be as calm and as sure of yourself as you can. A little nervousness before a test is normal.

Arrive at the exam room early in order to become adjusted to the setting. If possible, choose a seat away from others where you will not be disturbed. Avoid other students who may be jittery and talk negatively about the exam. Concentrate on the job at hand, and review any items that are very difficult for you to remember and which you intend to write on your paper the moment you receive the test.

In the final ten minutes before the test, clear your mind of all distractions. Relax, smile, and be sure you have all the pens, pencils, and paper you will need.

TAKING A WRITTEN TEST

When you receive the test, immediately write the difficult items you have been memorizing in an inconspicuous place on your paper. You will find that this builds your confidence because you have the most difficult items ready to use when needed.

Now read the instructions slowly and carefully. Rushing at this point could be disastrous. If you don't follow the instructions, there is little chance you will be rewarded for your long, hard preparation. After reading the instructions, take time to prepare your strategy or "game plan." Note the amount of time available and decide on the best use of this time. Suppose you have fifty minutes to complete a test that contains some questions that can be answered with a single word, and one question that is a 100-word translation. You might decide to allot fifteen minutes for the one-word answers and the remainder of the time for the translation. The value and difficulty level of each item is important. It is unwise to use twenty minutes to answer in detail a question worth ten points, and then have only ten minutes left to answer a question worth thirty points.

Complete all the easy items first, then return to the more difficult items. Doing this should help build your confidence, and while responding to the easy items, you may recall information that can help you answer the difficult items. Even when you have little idea about how to respond to an item, supply some sort of answer. You could receive partial credit for a farfetched response, but you can never receive credit for leaving an item blank.

As you become proficient in your new language, you will probably be asked to write essay responses. In order to use your time efficiently, write the major and minor ideas you wish to develop in the margin of your paper, and use this mini-outline to help compose your essay. Fill in your outline as quickly as possible so that you are sure to finish in the allotted time. After you have drafted your essay, edit it for grammar and spelling.

Two ideas should be kept in mind while writing a test. One is that you will probably not know all the answers. The other is that your instructor probably understands the time constraints, knows what is reasonable to expect at your level of proficiency, and will evaluate your responses accordingly.

TAKING AN ORAL TEST

If you are tested orally, use conversational management techniques. Slow down conversations by asking for something to be repeated or said in a different way. Learn how to check out what you think you heard; ask "Are you saying that. . .?" or "Do you mean. . .?" Find out if it is acceptable to use your native language to obtain clarification or to keep the conversation moving. Your aim is to communicate, and you cannot be expected to know absolutely all the words you might need. However, your instructor will probably expect you to use vocabulary you have practiced in class. Knowing these words should increase your confidence.

ASSESSING YOUR PERFORMANCE

Students often get together after a test for a postmortem. If you do this, keep in mind that the answers discussed at this point may not be the correct ones. Meeting with other learners immediately after a test can be a positive learning experience, but it doesn't make sense to believe everything you hear. If you believe you have done poorly, don't dwell on the subject and don't berate yourself. It's more profitable to use your energies in other ways.

When your test has been graded and returned, assess your performance carefully. Find your problem areas and be sure the instructor supplies the correct answers and explains the evaluation of your test to your satisfaction. If your instructor does not return your test, make arrangements to review it in the instructor's office. A careful analysis of each test will help you plan your future test strategies.

TAKING STANDARDIZED TESTS

Everything that has been said so far about tests applies to classroom tests devised by an instructor for a particular class. At some time, however, you may take a local or national standardized test. These tests are designed by examiners who neither know you personally nor know what you have been doing in your class. Standardized tests are often used to determine your proficiency level for placement into a language course, to assess your progress at the end of a course, or to determine your capability for handling the requirements of a particular job in a second language. Most standardized tests are of the paper-and-pencil, multiple-choice variety because they are easy to score. They also may include taped oral questions requiring written responses.

A standardized test typically contains more items than anyone can answer within the time limit, so that speed, as well as accuracy, is part of the scoring. The questions range from easy to very difficult, so few people will be able to answer all of them. You need to be aware of this so that you are not discouraged when you discover that the test is much harder than any you have taken before. The items on standardized tests have been tried out with thousands of people, and only those items that have been proved to correlate with other measures of proficiency are used on the actual tests.

When you take a standardized test, find out whether points are deducted from your score for wrong answers. If they are, you should answer only those items you are sure of and leave the rest blank. If there is no penalty for a wrong guess, you should answer every item. When you reach the point where there is one minute left, arbitrarily choose a response and answer all items not yet answered.

It is often possible to obtain a good score on a standardized test with a very small percentage of correct answers. For example, at one college where the College Board Achievement Test in foreign language is used for placement, you can place into the second semester course by answering correctly only about ten percent of the items!

More and more, oral interviews are replacing or supplementing paper-and-pencil tests as proficiency measures. These interviews usually last from five minutes to a half hour, and are conducted following defined procedures which assure you the same score no matter who interviews you. They are designed to find the highest level at which you can function orally in your second language. The examiner tries to determine your interests as well as your knowledge of the language so that the interview can be individualized to let you show yourself off at your best. For this reason, most people leave these interviews with a very positive feeling about themselves and their performance.

SUMMARY

Efficient preparation for tests, elimination of test anxiety, and the development of appropriate strategies for use during written and oral tests can give you confidence in your ability to succeed and to demonstrate this ability to your instructor and to yourself.

Several resources that are external to yourself, your new language, and your instructor are available to help you succeed. Chapter 9 will introduce you to the countless technological learning aids on the market, as well as to some that are still on the drawing board!

9

Technological Aids

In today's world there are several technological innovations that can enhance the study of your new language. These include public and commercial television, radio, cassettes and records, videotapes, and computers. These aids are worthwhile as learning tools only in relation to the value of the materials used with them. Most of the software programs used with computers, as well as most recorded materials, are not effective when used *by themselves* to teach languages. However, some innovations which are now in experimental stages hold great promise as supplements to books, teachers, and face-to-face language experiences.

RADIO AND TELEVISION

Provided you have the necessary listening ability, foreign language broadcasts on radio and television offer you opportunities to hear in your new language the same programs that native speakers hear. At first, you may be able to understand only the weather reports on TV, but soon you will understand the main ideas of the news when you have already heard the news in your native language. Commercials are usually easy to understand, especially when the products are familiar. Most radio programs are too difficult for beginning language learners, since the visual cues that aid understanding on television and in face-to-face communication are not available on the radio. If your proficiency is more advanced, radio and TV programs can help extend your knowledge of culture, add to your vocabulary, and develop listening skills. By recording programs on an audiotape or videotape recorder, you can hear programs more than once.

It is a good idea to find out what foreign language broadcasts can be received in your area. Almost every area has some locally originated ethnic programming on either radio or TV. In the northeastern United States, French-language broadcasts from Quebec can be received; and in the south and southwest, transmissions in Spanish from Mexico and Cuba are easy to find. The Spanish International Network (SIN) can now be seen on television in most areas of the U.S. Shortwave radio allows you to tune in to the world's airwaves, and satellite dishes are beginning to offer the same possibilities for television. If your new language is one that is difficult to find on normal broadcasting channels, you should inquire whether a nearby library or university has a satellite dish that could enable you to view distant television broadcasts.

Because radio and television are one-way communicators that do not provide the interaction necessary for language acquisition, their use in learning a new language is limited. As more knowledge is gained about language acquisition, special programs designed as a supplement to other language learning activities may appear on television in the near future.

RECORDS AND CASSETTES

Because of their size and because they can be used to hear, but not record, a new language at home, phonograph records are used less frequently for language learning. Nevertheless, foreign language materials on records are still available in libraries and bookstores. Most materials designed to aid language learning are recorded on audiocassettes. With both forms of recording, a good idea—in addition to following the instructions in the program—is to try to write down, word for word, what you hear. This will provide some evidence of your comprehension. And if a written script accompanies the recorded materials, you will be able to check what you have written. Remember, however, that you do not need to understand every single word in order to comprehend the spoken language.

You may use your cassette recorder to record lectures, broadcasts, and your own voice. And with the new, portable cassette players, you can listen to cassettes while you are commuting, exercising, or doing household tasks. The use of your cassette recorder is limited primarily by your imagination, and your learning will be enhanced by its use.

VIDEOTAPES

Foreign films are available on videotape and can be used to advantage by learners whose proficiency is beyond the novice stage. Some materials specifically designed to aid language learning are also available. The British Broadcasting Corporation (BBC) series, which were originally broadcast on television, is a notable example.[1] Available for French, German, Greek, Russian, and Spanish, these tapes combine traditional language instruction with serial adventure stories filmed on location in the appropriate countries. The cost of a complete set of videotapes for even one language is, unfortunately, beyond the reach of most individuals, so you would have to use them at a library or school.

COMPUTERS

Computers at work, school, and home are part of modern life. In the near future, they are certain to be part of language learning. Most of the software that has been marketed for foreign language learning so far has been very similar to what is found in textbooks; and while computer programs are more expensive than books, they are also more interesting for some people. You may find that you are more motivated to study by working with a computer, and you may be able to stay alert through a software drill more easily than if you sat at your desk and studied a book.

Artificial intelligence—that is, the capacity of the computer to store information about your responses and to tailor materials automatically to your needs—offers the likelihood that future software will be very different from traditional textbook materials for learning languages. Computers can be programmed to recognize a variety of appropriate responses to instructions, to ''converse'' with you, to keep records of your strengths and weaknesses in your new language, and to provide opportunities to work on precisely the areas of the language that you most need. Researchers who understand both the language acquisition process and computer systems are developing exciting programs that should represent a giant step forward in language learning aids.

LASER VIDEODISCS

Trying to find a particular place on an audiocassette or a videocassette is a cumbersome process. Laser videodiscs, connected to computers, avoid this limitation because the computer can access instantly any point on the disc, move forward or backward, or freeze an image on a screen. This expensive technology has been used in military and commercial training and is beginning to be applied in language learning. The learner watches a lesson on a TV monitor; at an appropriate point, the image freezes and a question is asked either orally or in writing. The learner is given a set of responses from which to choose. The consequences of each response have been recorded on the laser disc, and when the computer receives a response from the learner, it plays the portion of the disc that conveys to the learner the consequence of the response. Just as in real life, the learner remembers what happened and may modify responses to future problems.

A project known as Montevidisco has been developed at Brigham Young University to aid in learning Spanish. The user sees on a screen the village in Mexico where the materials were actually recorded and hears the conversation of the villagers. A villager asks a question, and the image freezes until the learner chooses a response. Depending on the choice, the program continues with an appropriate next scene. This system is like an adventure game because the sequence of events depends on the learner's responses. Both language and cultural skills are practiced as the learner concentrates on continuing the journey through the village.

As the cost of laser discs decreases, this technology will be combined with the computer's other capacities in the development of the most exciting and innovative aids to language learning yet devised. The possibilities are indeed beyond our imagination.

TECHNOLOGY AND YOU

You need to be aware of the rapid changes and advances in technology which may offer you opportunities to further the learning of your new language. As a consumer, you should ask several questions about these expensive materials before deciding to invest time or money in them. If the questions on the following checklist can be answered "yes," then the materials are likely to be effective.

1. Do the materials involve meaningful dialogue between you and the computer or other people?

2. Is the initiative for reacting to the computer in your hands? In other words, do you have to find out what the computer knows?

3. Are you immersed in the new language without reference to your native language?

4. When you have problems, does the program provide for interaction with an instructor away from the computer setting?

5. Is the program linked to other activities so that the work done with machines is only part of your total learning? Is there an opportunity for person-to-person contact?

SUMMARY

This chapter has suggested ways to use technological aids in the study of your new language. Since changes in technology occur so rapidly, it will never be possible to describe everything that is in existence at a given time. Therefore, it is necessary for you to be able to evaluate technological aids with the understanding that machines are unlikely to replace the personal interaction needed to develop proficiency in your new language. However, they do offer the potential for interesting and productive experiences that go beyond the capacity of books.

10

Survival and Success

Beginning the study of a new language is usually an exciting, stimulating experience, but as the months go by, the excitement often wanes, and you may wonder if you can survive long enough to reach your goals. A few learners know what they want to accomplish; they study efficiently and reach their goals. However, many language learners experience periods of time when survival and success seem unreachable. Two reasons for this are that their goals may have changed or that they do not know the techniques for survival. Survival depends on various personal, environmental, and educational factors—such as motivation; the need to succeed; commitment of time, money, and energy; and the availability and relevance of courses. If you have doubts about continuing to study your new language, you may find that reassessing your commitment will help you survive and succeed. If you have come to a crossroads in your language study, the following questionnaire is designed to help you decide what to do next.

YOUR NEXT STEPS

A. Have you reached the goals you established when you
   set out to learn your new language?   Yes   No

If the answer to *A* is "Yes," congratulations! You know how to survive and succeed, and you need not continue with this questionnaire. If you circled "No," read on.

B. Have your goals changed?   Yes   No

If the answer to *B* is "Yes," reassess your goals using the
questionnaire in Chapter 1. If you circled "No," continue.

C. Do you really want or need to continue studying?   Yes   No

   Are you willing to continue your commitment of time,
   energy, and money in order to reach your goals?   Yes   No

If you circled at least one "Yes" in *C,* continue to *D.* Otherwise,
read the section of this chapter entitled "Ending Your Study."

D. Do you need help with. . .
   1. motivation?   Yes   No
   2. procrastination?   Yes   No
   3. moving off a learning plateau?   Yes   No
   4. study skills?   Yes   No

If you answered "Yes" to 1, 2, or 3, this chapter will present you
with several good ideas. If you answered "Yes" to 4, reread
Chapters 3, 4, and 6 as well as the present chapter.

E. Have you explored all possible learning options?
   1. Total immersion programs?   Yes   No
   2. Individual coaching?   Yes   No
   3. Private language schools?   Yes   No
   4. Self-study?   Yes   No
   5. College courses?   Yes   No
   6. Public school adult classes?   Yes   No

Further ideas about these options are found in Chapter 2.

ENDING YOUR STUDY

   A decision to end the formal part of your study of your new language means either you have reached your original goals, or you no
longer have the need or the desire to pursue them. For both younger
students and adults, finding time to study may be difficult; yet you
have not wasted your time because you have gained some knowl-

edge of a new language. This knowledge may prove useful to you at a later time, and some day you may decide to study again. Although you may not engage in formal study activities, you can continue to speak, read, and write in your new language whenever the opportunity arises. By using your new language informally, you will retain much of what you know and will probably add to your knowledge.

LEARNING TO SUCCEED

The remainder of this chapter offers ways to motivate yourself to learn, to overcome procrastination, and to move yourself off a learning plateau. Understanding these problem areas should help you to survive and succeed in reaching your goals.

MOTIVATING YOURSELF FOR SUCCESS

How do you motivate yourself to keep studying and learning after the initial novelty and excitement of a new language have worn off? Motivation is based on the depth of your intellectual interest and/or personal need to learn. If you need to learn your new language for a job promotion, you are likely to be more motivated than if you attend a class because friends suggested you accompany them. Some people discover that they love the intellectual challenge of foreign language study, and the challenge itself becomes the motivating factor.

Many people, however, need to set up artificial motivational factors in order to make themselves study. The first of these factors is the clear definition of large and small goals. For many learners, structured courses help define goals, and the exams and assignments that are part of class attendance constitute short-term goals and provide motivation through a reward system such as grades. It is very important to note that none of the factors mentioned so far has to do with the new language itself nor with the possibility of using the language for practical purposes. If you can set your goals in terms of personal use of your new language, you will create the strongest possible motivating factors.

You can make your own study periods interesting and motivating and thus assure that your studies are intrinsically interesting. To avoid boring yourself while studying, vary your study techniques by miming, talking into a mirror, and making tape recordings. When you have long assignments, include physical exercise, such as aerobics, in your study period. If you make your study times interesting, you will look forward to them, your motivation will increase, and you will discover that foreign language study is pleasurable.

Another motivational factor involves rewarding yourself for the goals you have achieved. As you look forward to the reward, you will be motivated to keep trying and to succeed. For example, Jo Ann sometimes rewards herself with an ice-cream cone after memorizing a group of new words. When she completes a paper or passes a difficult exam, she may buy herself something she really wants, such as a new sweater. As she sweats away the long study hours, she keeps her rewards in mind and has discovered that they help to keep her motivated toward her goals. You, too, will find that a personal reward system combined with clearly defined goals and the development of interesting study activities in your new language will motivate you to succeed.

PROCRASTINATION

Procrastination is putting off until later some relatively small tasks directly related to the accomplishment of your long-term goals. For example, suppose you had planned to study, but you can't concentrate; so you decide to escape to a more pleasurable activity—phoning a friend, reading a magazine, daydreaming, or even making lists of things you need to do. If you do this often, you are teaching yourself that accomplishing nothing should be rewarded with pleasurable activity. If you reward yourself for nonaccomplishments, you will never get your work done. In order to change your behavior, you have to reward productive work with pleasurable activity and not reward unproductive behavior. To start, set a goal you know you can accomplish, such as memorizing ten words in fifteen minutes. If ten words are too many, set an easier goal. When you finish, reward yourself with a cookie or a jog around the block.

As you work to become a productive learner, you may feel that you can't accomplish everything you set out to do. Setting attainable goals, carrying them out, and giving yourself rewards takes practice. At first, reward yourself for accomplishing most of what you intended to do. As your ability to attain small goals increases, raise your standards. You will soon be in control of your learning!

LEARNING PLATEAUS

At the beginning of your language study, you may learn rapidly; but as you continue to study, you may reach a learning plateau. When you are at a learning plateau, a long time appears to go by without much evidence of learning, change, or progress. As an adult, you may find this discouraging and believe the task is too difficult for you. It is helpful to know that plateaus are times of mental consolidation and are part of normal learning experiences.

Still, there are several things you can try which may get you moving off a plateau. Assess your goals. Are they realistic? Unrealistic goals may make your task impossible; therefore, set goals you can reach. Perhaps you need to use different study techniques, or perhaps if you just keep working patiently, you will move ahead. If you have been sick or have personal problems that prevent you from learning, you are likely to remain on a plateau until these difficulties are resolved.

If you are on a plateau for an extended period of time, your whole approach to studying may be inappropriate. For instance, you may be using the wrong modality for learning. Perhaps you are concentrating on an oral approach; whereas if you used a combination of modalities, you could learn more easily. Perhaps you are in a class in which the procedure used by the instructor does not suit your learning style. Quite simply, you may need to find another type of class. You might find that individualized coaching will help you over your problem. Although individualized coaching is usually more expensive than other types of study, the one-on-one contact is an excellent way to move off a learning plateau. A few sessions with a coach may be all that you need. Good sources of coaches are high school teachers and graduate students at your local university. Native speakers of your new language are a possibility, although often they are not trained to identify your specific problem or to use your first language to explain concepts.

SURVIVAL

Whether you are an adult working full-time at an outside job, a homemaker, or a full- or part-time college student, you have special concerns which may affect the learning of your new language. The following sections address these needs and offer some suggestions for keeping your head above water.

SURVIVAL FOR ADULTS WHO WORK FULL-TIME

For an adult with a full-time job or full-time home responsibilities, survival in foreign language study may at times be tenuous. When you have to meet the needs of others as well as your own, stress can quickly escalate. For example, you may need a new language to function on the job, and your boss may expect you to do well in the language. Meanwhile, you have all your usual job and home responsibilities to deal with, as well as the unexpected things that happen. These situations can slow down your learning. Realizing that setbacks are common to everyone in your position can help you prepare for these realities. Try to think of your setbacks as temporary situations, and get back into your study routines as soon as possible. If you have difficulty doing this, seek help! Your instructor or a counselor may be able to offer useful suggestions.

The major survival problem faced by adults is discouragement. Discouragement arises when you do not reach goals on schedule, do not perform as well as some of your younger classmates, or encounter conflicts due to work and home-related activities. Some of these difficulties can be resolved through careful planning, but others must be accepted and lived with.

> John was beginning his second year of language study and was pleased with his progress because he was hoping for a promotion to an international office in his company. Then he and his wife had a new baby with physical problems requiring around-the-clock nursing care. John was so overwhelmed by his new responsibilities that he could not continue with his language study. When the baby's problems were resolved, he was finally able to resume his studies.

Though at first John felt terribly discouraged, resuming his study schedule provided him with a feeling of control. He set his goal of promotion a year farther into the future and adjusted his thinking to the realities of adult life.

You, too, can survive disappointment and discouragement by changing original goals to meet the realities of life, and understanding that adults can study and succeed, but the process may take longer than expected.

Not doing as well as classmates may be a source of discouragement, especially if the classmates are much older or younger than you. Age provides both advantages and disadvantages for learners. Adult learners usually do as well as, if not better than, younger students when reasoning and decision-making skills are involved. In memorization, younger learners seem to have an advantage. Because successful learning of your new language requires memorization, you may need to accept the fact that you will memorize more slowly than some others. If you memorize daily and follow your time management plans, your regular study habits should repay you richly, and you should then be able to keep up with those who are younger. If you find you cannot keep up, make adjustments in your plans to allow additional time for memorization. Avoid discouragement by rewarding yourself for reaching small goals, and as the months go by, your concern with memorization should diminish, and your success with memorization is likely to increase.

SURVIVAL FOR COLLEGE STUDENTS

Beginning college students sometimes face problems related to their lack of experience with college life. Suppose you are doing poorly in French, but you did not withdraw from the course during the drop period allowed in your college catalog—what can you do? You know that foreign language learning is cumulative, and you believe you will fail the course because your cumulative knowledge is weak. You may consider not returning to class, and taking an *F* for the course. This is a decision you should never make on your own because you can never predict the factors that come into play when instructors calculate final grades. You need to think carefully before resigning yourself to a failure that may mean academic warning or may lead to dismissal from college. There are things you can do, even at the last minute, to help yourself. It is not wise to shrug your shoulders and stop going to class.

First of all, talk to your instructor and ask for study suggestions. Even if your instructor tells you it is too late, it is unwise to give up before checking all possibilities. If you have been under stress or have difficulty understanding the reasons for your failure to learn, see a college counselor. A counselor can help you evaluate alternatives and may suggest some you hadn't thought of. In some colleges the counselor can recommend withdrawal without a grade penalty or an extension of time to complete the work.

At this crucial point, find out exactly what will be contained in the rest of the course. Gear all your study periods to this material. What have been your strong points in the course—vocabulary, translation, oral communication? Concentrate on the areas you learn best. Sometimes a tutor can do wonders for you, even at the last minute, and can help you identify exactly what you need to know in order to pass.

Let's suppose you really do fail and get an *F.* It is not the end of the world. Analyze what happened so you will not repeat the same tactical mistakes. When you retake the course, try to select a different instructor. Even if the instructor had nothing to do with your failure, you will get a fresh start and a new approach to learning your language.

SUCCESS

Success in language study means different things to different people. For most individuals, minimal success is the ability to understand and speak a new language well enough to survive in a country where the language is spoken, and to read signs, notices, and newspapers. As you work toward reaching your original language learning goals, you will discover that goals tend to extend, change emphasis, and present new and unexpected challenges. By using the ideas in this book, you can develop your ability to learn languages successfully, and language learning becomes a growing, challenging part of your life. Yes! You can learn a foreign language.

Notes

Chapter 1

1. The levels of proficiency are more completely described in *ACTFL Proficiency Guidelines* (Hastings-on-Hudson, NY: American Council on the Teaching of Foreign Languages, 1982). This booklet, which may be obtained from the Council, contains specific examples of how people speak, understand, read, and write at each level in French, German, and Spanish, as well as descriptions of the cultural knowledge appropriate at each level.

   For the most recent guidelines, containing additional information about the proficiency levels, see *Defining and Developing Proficiency: Guidelines, Implementations, and Concepts*, Heidi Byrnes and Michael Canale, eds. (Lincolnwood, IL: National Textbook Co., 1986).

2. Arthur P. Sorenson, Jr., "Multilingualism in the Northwest Amazon," *American Anthropologist* 69 (1967): 670-84

Chapter 5

1. Betty Lou Leaver, "Twenty Minutes to Mastery of the Cyrillic Alphabet," *Foreign Language Annals* 17 (1984): 215-20.

2. Zev Bar-lev, "Hebrew Hieroglyphics," *Visible Language* 17 (1983): 365-79.

3. J. L. Laychuk, "The Use of Etymology and Phonetic Symbols (zhùyīn fúhaò) in Teaching First Year Chinese." Arlington, VA: ERIC Document Reproduction Service, NO. ED 240 840, 1983.

Chapter 9

1. The U.S. distributor of the BBC series is Films Incorporated,
   1144 Wilmette Avenue, Wilmette, IL 60091.

Appendix A
A Word to Counselors
and Teachers

Counselors and teachers have the role of encouraging, motivating, and helping students in their language learning. The study skills detailed in this book can provide ideas for helping those who are beginning to learn a new language and may be used with individuals or groups to hasten and improve learning. Counselors also have influence over students' language choices and over their attitudes toward language learning. Peer and community beliefs influence choices and attitudes, but counselors' and teachers' advice is very important because they are the professionals to whom learners turn for guidance whether they are adults, college students, or high school students. Because we live in an international society in which the barriers to interaction between peoples are constantly being eliminated, knowledge of languages is a pressing social and economic priority. Counselors and teachers have in their hands a major part of the responsibility for encouraging successful language learning.

Counselors can discover, through such sources as interviews and questionnaires, the attitudinal and motivational factors in students' lives that will help them choose suitable languages and study successfully. Motivation for language study is both instrumental and integrative. *Instrumental motives* are factors external to the learners themselves, such as requirements for degrees, diplomas, or employment; or the desire to please someone else. On the other hand, a person with *integrative motivation* wants to study for personal reasons including intellectual desire, curiosity, and interest in becoming more like the speakers of the new language. People who study a language for instrumental reasons often do not do as well as people who learn for integrative reasons because their motivation does not come from within themselves. It is therefore important for counselors to help each learner find true personal reasons for wanting to study. If a person begins language study for instrumental reasons, counselors should provide support so the learner becomes so intrigued by the experience that motivation becomes integrative.

Language study encompasses a lifetime of learning inside and outside the classroom. Enrolling in one language course is just the beginning of language acquisition and learning. Learners need to obtain a vision of what can be done with a foreign language, both economically and socially, by planning with a counselor for the potential future use of their new language. In this way people come to understand the long-term value of language learning and become enthusiastic language learners.

Counselors have been known to recommend German and French to bright students, and Spanish to weaker students, on the supposition that the latter language is easier. The only linguistic basis for supposing that anyone would have an easier time with Spanish is the fact that Spanish spelling corresponds quite closely to pronunciation, which is not the case with French. German spelling and sound also correspond closely, but German vocabulary contains fewer similarities to English, and therefore the demands on a learner's memory may be slightly greater than for the Romance languages. Aside from these linguistic observations, popular determinations of the relative difficulty of languages are most probably based on cultural stereotypes which have no basis in reality. Successful language acquisition depends primarily on the learner's attitude and motivation, and it is these factors that counselors should consider in recommending one language or another.

In colleges and high schools, counselors can help the development of interest in foreign languages by reaching out to offer services such as study skills workshops, stress avoidance seminars, seminars for adult reentry students, as well as workshops for faculty to help them with the problem learners. Newsletters and notices in school publications may increase faculty and student awareness of these services, and cooperative efforts between counselors and faculty can provide strong support for foreign language study.

Once a learner is enrolled in a class, the way in which language instruction is approached is likely to be a major factor in motivating learning. Just as different people learn in different ways, there are many effective styles of language teaching. The most effective language instruction is aimed at helping people to communicate with others. The goal is to learn to use the language in real-life settings, and the teacher's role is to develop ideas for these settings. Emphasis is on comprehension, and role playing is often used because it enables students to create realistic dialogues. Vocabulary and verb forms are memorized in meaningful contexts. The new language is used as much as possible by the instructor, and learners begin to speak in the new language when they feel confident to do so. Language acquisition takes place in an atmosphere of freedom to make errors without correction, so the classroom becomes a place for the learner to experiment with the new language without being put ''on the spot.''

Counselors and teachers can best help foreign language learners by encouraging them to form positive, realistic attitudes toward the task of language learning and toward their new language and its culture, and by providing an environment in which a learner's language acquisition ability can flourish.

Appendix B
Recommended Reading

ON THE VALUE OF FOREIGN LANGUAGES

Huebner, Theodore. *Opportunities in Foreign Language Careers,* revised edition. Lincolnwood, IL: National Textbook Co., 1981.

This book discusses educational preparation, specific steps for getting started in finding a job, and careers in foreign trade and government.

Simon, Paul. *The Tongue-Tied American: Confronting the Foreign Language Crisis.* New York: Continuum, 1980.

The U.S. Senator from Illinois documents convincingly what is lost to the United States because of the lack of foreign language proficiency on the part of its citizens.

ON FOREIGN LANGUAGE LEARNING

Krashen, Stephen D. *Principles and Practice in Second Language Acquisition.* Oxford: Pergamon Press, 1982.

Today's most outstanding specialist in second language learning defines a theory according to which the best ways of learning languages are also the most enjoyable.

Oskarsson, Mats. *Approaches to Self-Assessment in Foreign Language Learning.* Oxford: Pergamon Press, 1980.

This slim volume suggests ways in which adults can assess their own progress in their new language.

Rubin, Joan, and Irene Thompson. *How to Be a More Successful Language Learner.* Boston: Heinle & Heinle, 1982.

This book describes various strategies used by successful language learners.

Stevick, Earl W. *Memory, Meaning, and Method: Some Psychological Perspectives on Language Learning.* Rowley, MA: Newbury House, 1976.
This well-written book outlines, in a clear and entertaining way, technical evidence of the relationship between memory and personal involvement in language learning.

ON STUDY SKILLS

Apps, Jerold W. *Study Skills for Adults Returning to School,* second edition. New York: McGraw-Hill, 1982.
This problem-solving book, focused on the adult learner, provides tips for success and dispels myths about age and the ability to learn.

Kagan, Corin E. *Coping with College: The Efficient Learner.* New York: McGraw-Hill, 1982.
An undergraduate reveals strategies for college success.

Lakein, Alan. *How to Get Control of Your Time and Your Life.* New York: New American Library, 1973.
Learning a new language can be time-consuming; suggestions made in this book can help learners set priorities and accomplish goals.

Pauk, Walter. *How to Study in College,* third edition. Boston: Houghton Mifflin, 1984.
Chapters on concentration, forgetting and remembering, and vocabulary are especially relevant to learning a new language.

Index

ABOUT THE AUTHORS

MARJORY BROWN-AZAROWICZ has a Ph.D. in counseling and reading education from the University of Washington. At George Mason University, she is a professor of education, specializing in the teaching of reading to high school students and those with bilingual backgrounds. She is the author of five books and many articles.

MARK G. GOLDIN received a Ph.D. in linguistics from Georgetown University. He has taught English as a foreign language in Spain, and he has taught Spanish at Indiana University, the University of Colorado, Middlebury College, and Georgetown University, in addition to George Mason University, where he is associate professor. His special interest is adult second language acquisition, and he has also written about Spanish linguistics.

CHARLOTTE MURISON STANNARD holds an M.Ed. in guidance and counseling in higher education from George Mason University, where she now works for the university's counseling center as coordinator of learning skills programs and programs for reentry students.

Edward Free
4654 Sharp Shooter Way
Prescott, AZ 86301

LANGUAGE AND TRAVEL BOOKS
FROM PASSPORT BOOKS

Dictionaries and References
Vox Spanish and English Dictionaries
Harrap's Concise Spanish and English
  Dictionary
Harrap's French and English Dictionaries
Klett German and English Dictionary
Harrap's Concise German and English
  Dictionary
Everyday American English Dictionary
Beginner's Dictionary of American
  English Usage
Diccionario Inglés
El Diccionario del Español Chicano
Diccionario Básico Norteamericano
British/American Language Dictionary
The French Businessmate
The German Businessmate
The Spanish Businessmate
Harrap's Slang Dictionary (French and English)
English Picture Dictionary
French Picture Dictionary
Spanish Picture Dictionary
German Picture Dictionary
Guide to Spanish Idioms
Guide to German Idioms
Guide to French Idioms
Guide to Correspondence in Spanish
Guide to Correspondence in French
Español para los Hispanos
Business Russian
Yes! You Can Learn a Foreign Language
Everyday Japanese
Japanese in Plain English
Korean in Plain English
Robin Hyman's Dictionary of Quotations
NTC's American Idioms Dictionary
Passport's Japan Almanac
Japanese Etiquette and Ethics in
  Business
How To Do Business With The Japanese
Korean Etiquette And Ethics In Business

Verb References
Complete Handbook of Spanish Verbs
Spanish Verb Drills
French Verb Drills
German Verb Drills

Grammar References
Spanish Verbs and Essentials of Grammar
Nice 'n Easy Spanish Grammar
French Verbs and Essentials of Grammar
Nice 'n Easy French Grammar
German Verbs and Essentials of Grammar
Nice 'n Easy German Grammar
Italian Verbs and Essentials of Grammar
Essentials of Russian Grammar

Welcome Books
Welcome to Spain
Welcome to France
Welcome to Ancient Greece
Welcome to Ancient Rome

Language Programs
Just Listen 'n Learn: Spanish, French, Italian,
  German and Greek
Just Listen 'n Learn Plus: Spanish, French,
  and German
Practice & Improve Your . . . Spanish, French
  and German
Practice & Improve Your . . . Spanish, French and
  German PLUS
Japanese For Children
Basic French Conversation
Basic Spanish Conversation

Phrase Books
Just Enough Dutch
Just Enough French
Just Enough German
Just Enough Greek
Just Enough Italian
Just Enough Japanese
Just Enough Portuguese
Just Enough Scandinavian
Just Enough Serbo-Croat
Just Enough Spanish
Multilingual Phrase Book
International Traveler's Phrasebook

Language Game Books
Easy French Crossword Puzzles
Easy French Word Games and Puzzles
Easy Spanish Crossword Puzzles
Easy Spanish Word Games and Puzzles
Let's Learn About Series: Italy, France,
  Germany, Spain, America
Let's Learn Coloring Books In Spanish,
  French, German, Italian, And English

Humor in Five Languages
The Insult Dictionary: How to Give 'Em
  Hell in 5 Nasty Languages
The Lover's Dictionary: How to Be
  Amorous in 5 Delectable Languages

Technical Dictionaries
Complete Multilingual Dictionary of
  Computer Terminology
Complete Multilingual Dictionary of
  Aviation and Aeronautical Terminology
Complete Multilingual Dictionary of
  Advertising, Marketing and Communications
Harrap's French and English
  Business Dictionary
Harrap's French and English
  Science Dictionary

Travel
Nagel's Encyclopedia Guides
World at Its Best Travel Series
Runaway Travel Guides
Mystery Reader's Walking Guide: London
Japan Today
Japan at Night
Discovering Cultural Japan
Bon Voyage!
Business Capitals of the World
Hiking and Walking Guide to Europe
Frequent Flyer's Award Book
Ethnic London
European Atlas
Health Guide for International Travelers
Passport's Travel Paks: Britain, Italy,
  France, Germany, Spain
Passport's China Guides
On Your Own Series: Brazil, Israel
Spain Under the Sun Series: Barcelona, Toledo,
  Seville and Marbella

Getting Started Books
Introductory language books for Spanish,
  French, German and Italian.

For Beginners Series
Introductory language books for children
  in Spanish, French, German and Italian.

PASSPORT BOOKS
a division of *NTC Publishing Group*
4255 West Touhy Avenue
Lincolnwood, Illinois 60646-1975